The Beatles: *Sgt. Pepper's Lonely Hearts Club Band*

University Centre Barnsley

Telephone: 01226 | 644281 |

University of
HUDDERSFIELD

UniversityCentre
Barnsley

2166 BEA

Class No: 782 · 4~~12640266~~

Suffix: MOO

This book is to be returned on or before
the last date stamped below

05 FEB 2008

CAMBRIDGE MUSIC HANDBOOKS

GENERAL EDITOR   Julian Rushton

Cambridge Music Handbooks provide accessible introductions to major musical works.

Published titles

The Beatles: *Sgt. Pepper's Lonely Hearts Club Band*

Allan F. Moore

London College of Music and Media
at
Thames Valley University

CAMBRIDGE
UNIVERSITY PRESS

PUBLISHED BY THE PRESS SYNDICATE OF THE UNIVERSITY OF CAMBRIDGE
The Pitt Building, Trumpington Street, Cambridge CB2 1RP, United Kingdom

CAMBRIDGE UNIVERSITY PRESS
The Edinburgh Building, Cambridge CB2 2RU, United Kingdom
40 West 20th Street, New York, NY 10011-4211, USA
10 Stamford Road, Oakleigh, Melbourne 3166, Australia

First published 1997
Reprinted 1998 (twice)

Printed in the United Kingdom at the University Press, Cambridge

Typeset in 10.5/13pt Monophoto Ehrhardt   [SE]

A catalogue record for this book is available from the British Library

Library of Congress cataloguing in publication data

Moore, Allan F.
The Beatles, Sgt. Pepper's Lonely Hearts Club Band / Allan F.
Moore
p.   cm. – (Cambridge music handbooks)
Includes bibliographical references and index.
ISBN 0 521 57381 5 (hardback) – ISBN 0 521 57484 6 (paperback)
1. Beatles. Sgt. Pepper's Lonely Hearts Club Band.   2. Rock
music – England – History and criticism   I. Title.   II. Series.
ML421.B4M66   1997
782.42166'092'2–dc21   96–6714   CIP   MN

ISBN 0 521 57381 5 hardback
ISBN 0 521 57484 6 paperback

To Charlie,
greatest of friends

Contents

Preface

One Monday morning, during the summer of 1995, a hasty shopping trip was abruptly interrupted when I began to notice, to my great surprise, that more than half the music issuing from open shop doorways was by the Beatles and, of that, about half was music from *Sgt. Pepper's Lonely Hearts Club Band*. This is far from an authoritative sample, of course, but it did cause me to wonder why it is that this music, now largely thirty years old, has continued to exercise such a hold on the suburban provincial imagination, and not simply the imagination of those in their forties and fifties.

If I fully knew the answer to this, of course, I should be making records (and presumably money) rather than writing books. None the less, in what follows I shall map out some of the strands which went into the making of *Sgt. Pepper* and some of the paths which have developed from it, in the belief that the more closely we can engage with our subject, the closer we come to provisional answers to such questions.

There seems little doubt that, whatever the album's musical value (which I shall discuss in chapter 4), it has had a greater effect on the imagination of suburban British life than any other, partly for reasons surrounding its reception (which I shall discuss in chapter 5). Indeed, it has also probably had a more marked effect on academic musical life than any other single sample of 'pop' music, from Wilfrid Mellers's early review and his fuller subsequent discussion, through to Jonathan Dunsby's afterword to an earlier volume in this series, where he asks 'will a future dictionary of music have an entry for "*Sergeant Pepper*" somewhere between "Schoenberg" and "*Sprechstimme*"?'.[1] He asks the question in the context of ruminating on the survival value of Schoenberg's *Pierrot Lunaire* (written in 1912), in the midst of a century which has seen the very idea of a 'mainstream' attacked from all possible angles.

This becomes an extremely important point, for it concerns the problematic relationship between musical modernism and the music of mass culture, both of which (in their contradictory ways) are taken to be legitimate cultural expressions of modernity. I shall briefly explore this difficult ground in chapter 1, before offering a closer historical preparation for *Sgt. Pepper* in chapter 2.

The study of popular music is beset with particular problems not normally the concern of the student of concert, sacred or stage music. (Whether or not they should be is another matter.) The music's primary medium of transmission is the recording (whether tape, vinyl or compact disc) rather than the written or printed score. Not only this, but whatever sketches may have been made, they are equally likely to exist (if at all, which is unusual) on tape rather than on paper. Scribblings of lyrics often do exist, but at this point my concern is the musical settings for such lyrics. The closed archive at London's Abbey Road Studios (the site of almost all the Beatles' recording activities) does contain early mixes of much of their material, and I have had recourse to the work of both Lewisohn and Hertsgaard,[2] who have made some use of this material. I treat it rather briefly, however, for I am not convinced that it tells a particularly interesting story. Chapters 4 and 5 (analysis and reception of the album) are more extensive, for the same reason: the Beatles had no great tendency to write down sketches. The only thing we have approaching an authoritative score is, then, the recording itself. We do, of course, have a multitude of transcriptions, all made after the event, and to which commentators frequently make reference. I find this a problematic approach, if only because those elements which listeners tend to find most interesting in popular music and which most nearly capture the music's particular strengths (rhythmic and pitch nuance, texture, timbre) are impossible to notate accurately anyway, at least in the system inherited from Central European practice. Accordingly, I have assumed that readers of this book will have ready access to a recording which remains available thirty years after its origination. Instead of referring to bar numbers on a printed score, my detailed discussions will refer to CD timings, and to the lyrics which (for the first time in a popular music album) were printed on the record (and, subsequently, CD) sleeve. This is the surest way to guide your ear (rather than your eye) towards exactly what I am discussing at any particular point.

The absence of a score does not, however, mean that we have to forgo discussion of events which take place 'below the musical surface'. Because such events are always more concisely explained through music notation, I have made use, in chapter 4, of simple analytic reductions, particularly of harmonic patterns and medium-scale melodic contours. Although we know that the majority of listeners are unable to make explicit the effect such longer-term considerations have on their under-standings of and responses to songs, we also know from substitution tests that they do none the less have such effects. Indeed, they enhance our understanding of what the songs mean and, therefore, our self-understanding through explicating our responses.

My thanks are due to a number of people for the fact that this book has reached its present form. Martin Ellerby, David Gough and Peter Hunter kindly read through a final draft, while both Charlie Ford and Dai Griffiths will find many of their own suggestions thinly disguised; to both of them I am exceedingly grateful. The British Newspaper Library at Colindale provided access to many reviews. Both my editor, Julian Rushton, and Penny Souster at Cambridge University Press have been generous with their help and time: I hope their faith in this addition to the series has not been misplaced. Finally, to Sarah, Eleanor and our hi-fi, who alone know what they have to put up with: I promise I'll lay off the Beatles for a while.

I

Inheritance

In Europe, there has always been a popular culture: at least, that is, as long as there has been any other sort of culture (high, art, serious, aristocratic, sacred, etc.) from which to differentiate it. However, developments which can be dated to the nineteenth century totally changed the face of what we now experience as popular music. The music written by composers of Mozart's time differs remarkably little in style and tone in respect of its intended audience. By the time of the 'serious' piano waltzes of Chopin and Brahms, or that of Berlioz in the *Symphonie Fantastique*, a gap has clearly opened up in comparison with the waltzes of composers like Joseph Lanner, although concert programmes retained a mixture. By the turn of the present century this gap had become so large that the common origin of a century before could be totally overlooked. This situation would present no problem in itself, were it not for the fact that these now separating musical cultures were increasingly seen as oppositional to each other; hence the (unsuccessful) striving for an adequate term ('art', 'serious', 'classical') with which to oppose 'popular'. But such opposition is itself complicated by the fact that there is not *a* 'popular' music. Even simply put, by the time of Schoenberg's *Pierrot Lunaire*, we need to acknowledge certainly three rather than two cultural streams.

The first of these is 'popular culture', which scholars have interpreted in two different ways: either a culture dependent on an urban 'audience' (out of its historical roots in a folk 'community'), where the originators of an artefact (in our case, composers of a song or dance) are considered of secondary importance to its executors (its singers and players); or practices which resist the cultural hegemony either of high culture, or of mass culture. This latter meaning for 'popular' becomes particularly pertinent in the post-war period, as in the writings of cultural theorists.[1]

The second stream, 'mass culture', is usually considered a separate phenomenon, developed particularly in the USA by analogy with the factory system, where concepts of originality and individuality become greatly devalued. It was during the 1880s that the industry centred on Tin Pan Alley began, the very name conjuring visions of publishers' houses (e.g. the Brill Building) full of tiny rooms, each containing a piano, a lyricist and a composer, churning out ballads, love songs, dances, comedy songs, sentimental ditties and whatever the current fashion happened to be, and being paid by the song. Some would cite the non-modernist continuation of late Romanticism as representing a distinct (i.e. fourth) stream, but at least in its migration to Hollywood, it is sufficient for my simple initial purposes to site it here.

The third of these cultural streams, the 'modernist' developments of late Romanticism made by Schoenberg and others, has been interpreted as 'precisely an outraged and deliberately esoteric response to the new drive towards total commodification'. This total commodification is that mass culture represented by the development of centralized publishing systems (Tin Pan Alley in New York and Denmark Street in London), gramophone companies, radio and, later, the film industry, and is more familiar from art theory. In the post-war period, this 'response' which Middleton identifies has come to seem intrinsic. Georgina Born, for instance, argues that the rise of modernist formalism in the 1950s was founded on its non-negotiable, utter distinction from a 'popular' [*sic*] culture. Indeed, by that time, this 'other' culture was itself becoming as closed as that of the Darmstadt composers. In the years preceding and during the Second World War, 'popular music' covered a narrow spread of styles from theatre song, through Tin Pan Alley and Hollywood, to the remnants of vaudeville. It was in modes of consumption, rather than styles, that distinctions could be made. A yet-bleaker view is offered by Dave Harker, who argues that a very small number of people were in charge of commercial music, such that the audience becomes more or less a passive consumer. There were cases where the audience appeared to influence output by what they seemed to consume, but it was the industry's manipulation of the market which remained dominant.[2]

At the time, the opposition between these cultures was not discussed as such. Rather, it was only 'high art' which was recognized as 'culture', largely on the grounds that it could be considered autonomous from the workings of 'industry', 'commerce' or even 'society'. Its values were considered universal and transcendent and therefore beyond question. The distinction between this 'culture' and the workings of 'industry' or 'commerce' in the artistic field was strongly maintained, and those in positions of social power frequently claimed that the latter contained the permanent potential to 'level down' the former. Thus, at this time, the British record industry aimed its products entirely at a middle-class market, with non-negotiable categories: classical, jazz, dance, vocal. There was no other recognized market even in the early days of rock 'n' roll (individual artists would be pigeon-holed as 'dance' or 'vocal' or, occasionally, 'jazz', much as they are even today, although with an expansion in the range of categories). The big money was still being made in live performances, where the venue's name (and implicitly understood booking policy) was a far better guide to the pleasures on offer, and through the extensive network of London publishers and agents. Prior to 1914, music hall had been unchallenged in the UK as an entertainment venue, after which time 'variety', cinema, the gramophone and radio gradually replaced it. These new, electronic, media began the decline of live music making (who wants a piano when you can have a radio?) although a very limited amount of music was broadcast on the purist pre-war BBC. Of these media, recordings came to be the most important, while the development of the industry between the wars was based on its new-found ability to create its own formulaic repertory from the raw material of urban and ethnic musics. This industry was, of course, a US development, and the growth of British popular culture was, largely, as a US dependency.[3]

The influence of American popular culture on that of Britain increased with the presence of US forces in Britain between 1942 and 1945 and Forces Network radio, followed by the stirrings of media globalization and film heroes like Montgomery Clift, James Dean and Marlon Brando. By the mid-1950s, singers who had risen to fame through fronting swing bands had bequeathed the style of the popular singer: Frank Sinatra, Bing Crosby, Rosemary Clooney, Patti Page, Doris Day, Nat King Cole, Perry Como. When Elvis Presley burst upon the British scene in late 1956 with 'Heartbreak hotel', it seemed to the British (and much of the American) audience that this new, invigorating sound had come from nowhere. What was not known at the time was that

Presley's sound – his articulation, delivery, presence and accompaniment – was in large part the product of a long line of development of black musical styles. This ran chronologically parallel to that of the 'popular' *per se*, a development the tracing of which had huge consequences for the Beatles and their peers. To sketch this history briefly we must return to jazz, noting broad parallelisms between its recorded face in the USA and the UK.

The first 'jazz' record appeared in 1917, made by the Original Dixieland Jazz Band (a group of white New Orleans musicians of Italian extraction). By 1919 they were touring the UK. Subsequent stylistic innovations, particularly 'swing' in the late 1920s and the Dixieland revival (an anti-progressive, populist move) a decade or more later, were also current in Britain. One of the major figures in the latter was Chris Barber, whose 'Jazz and Blues Band' cut an album in 1954 containing two 'joke' songs sung by banjo player Tony (later Lonnie) Donegan, accompanied only by guitar, string bass and washboard. This was released as a single due to apparent public demand; by 1956 'skiffle' was born, a style which nurtured many musicians coming to the fore in the late 1950s, not least what would later become the Beatles, John Lennon's band 'The Quarrymen'. 'The people' were on to this development: between 1952 and 1955 the sales of record players trebled, thus sparking the change in 'listening culture' with which we are now all familiar; Donegan's 'Rock Island line' made the charts in the UK and the USA only months before 'Heartbreak hotel', and the music press belatedly began to reflect this trend by listing sales of recorded rather than sheet music. Despite this pressure on the record industry to recognize the immense new market created by the invention of the 'teenager', it remained conservative through to the end of the decade.

By the early 1950s, most dancehalls were catering for mature tastes: those in their teens would frequently feel out of place, while those in their fifties would probably feel at home. Prior to the advent of rock 'n' roll (*c.* 1954) 'teenagers' did not exist, and their construction as gendered (i.e. separately male and female) working-class beings was crucial. This was being made clear by a 1959 report, which emphasized that middle-class teenagers were either still at school or beginning their careers. As Harker notes, the accent was already on manipulation of the market by capitalist industry, a manipulation which frequently comes under scrutiny in the relationship between 'mass' culture and 'popular' culture. The emphasis on the newly financially-enfranchised teenager comes from a number of sources. Arthur Marwick notes that the new technologically driven high-wage society developing in the 1950s gave working-class youth a certain control over technologically developed popular culture. This pace of technological change opened a gulf between the new cultural practice and residual practices of older generations, a distinction which, on the surface, encouraged talk less of class than of generational difference. In the UK, particularly after 1957, full employment, an increase in levels of consumption and the development of the welfare state began to suggest that class divisions were no longer relevant, even at the very moment when class connotation was a crucial feature of the emergent teenager. Thus the paradox of British teenagers: their culture was essentially a separate phenomenon, and yet it depended for its existence on the spending power achieved through their affluence, necessarily gained by functioning as fully integrated members of economic society.[4]

Dick Bradley is less ambivalent about the British teenager's position. He suggests that the very coining of the term separated off the teenager from other aspects of life: by naming disaffected youth, and by calling attention to the teenager as a *consumer* (both male and female), rather than as any particular sort of *worker*, the establishment (the BBC and upmarket newspapers, educators, politicians) worked to neutralize the perceived danger. The term was, for Bradley, filled with 'discourses of affluence, classlessness, juvenile delinquency, promiscuity [etc.]', all of which called attention to the teenager's *difference*. But because this new teenager was not only different, but separate, its social identity could not be found within established structures, but had to be created anew. For this new audience, 1950s American popular culture formed an imaginary other world, whose unfettered expression enticed with its very promise of delicious danger, while the steady replacement of big bands with small groups (with particularized individual instrumental roles) aided listeners' identification with them.[5] For Bradley, not only did the size of the US entertainment industries enable their colonization of the British working-class market, but the stasis of the British media, from which teenagers were alienated anyway, meant that 'American' was identified as 'new' and, since British teenagers were 'new', as 'ours'.

Against the view that a new *Zeitgeist* was so developing, Richard Peterson has usefully argued, specifically with reference to the USA, that changes in cultural constraint were far more significant. Prior to 1950, radio and record industries had operated in competition. In the early 1950s radio had become unsuccessful as a national (US) medium, spawning many local stations each requiring cheap programming material. Thus drama, comedy shows and live music were lost, to be replaced by records. Record sales, in decline to 1949, rose sharply. DJs on new radio stations acted not as functionaries, but as active compilers of the new radio-as-jukebox format. Thus the supposed homogeneous market of 1948 broke down into tiny local markets (each with a mosaic approach catering to different types of local needs) by a decade later. In a very short space of time, between late 1954 and early 1957, the new stylistic practices were formed as new 45 rpm records and independent distributors broke the oligopoly of the US music industry, committed as it still was to big band music.[6]

So not only is the teenager ambivalently situated between culture and economics, but the birth of teenage culture may well have been an extra-cultural event. And the contradictions continue. Teenage culture protested against established society and the organized music industry (represented by a previous generation of singers), while the developing consumer society required a constant infusion of the new. This 'new' was identified totally with youth as consumers (the teenager), whose identity was not bound up with what was already proven. Hence the vast availability of fashion, cosmetics, transistors, records. This protest was nevertheless founded on that society, and teenage culture became a massive commercial enterprise. The real degree of teenage disaffection is hard to determine. In the US, opposition to rock 'n' roll carried strong racial overtones. Rock 'n' roll posed a threat to the established record industry and its conservative attitudes, just as later it would to the entire British establishment. In the UK, disaffection was probably more assumed than actual: scenes of 'uproar' were reported in 1956 during showings of the film *Rock Around the Clock* (celebrating the music of the staid Bill Haley in particular), but by the following year rock 'n' roll had even become respectable,[7] with no hint of the US racial motive. In the longer term, the UK's growing affluence (of which the teenager as unencumbered consumer was very much the spearhead) enabled a general-ized sense of social revolt in tandem with the change from dreams of elegance where teenage years were simply those spent in repression of sexual feelings waiting for adulthood, to those of teenage romance where such feelings became the source of immediate pleasure.

Two further ambivalences are cited by Marwick. Although teenage culture contained a strong participatory element, it was none the less bound up with electronics. Marwick's assumption here concerns the (financial) elitism of electronic devices. And yet many bands began with a simple amplifier (for all three guitars), making use of the venue's PA (or equivalent) system to amplify voices. It is not until the period from 1966 to about 1975 (and the birth of punk) that the financial outlay required for extensive amplification and electronic gadgetry became critically important. Secondly, although the culture had innovative elements, 'high culture' critics still insist it spawned repetitive trivia. This remains an overworked point of criticism, for definitions of repetition betray the ideological investment of the definer. This issue is more fully treated in chapter 4.

In broad outline, then, this was the socio-musical environment in which that first generation of teenagers, who included in their number John Lennon and Richard Starkey (*b.* 1940), Paul McCartney (*b.* 1942) and George Harrison (*b.* 1943), found themselves. What they did with it, and how they moulded it into that place where *Sgt. Pepper* was to flourish, is the subject of the next chapter.

2

Preparation

When the Beatles formally began their recording career on 6 June 1962, Lennon and McCartney had been playing together intermittently for five years, while Harrison (then aged only fifteen) had joined what was 'John's group' a year later, in 1958. That long apprenticeship began with various gigs in Liverpool, but it was in the summer of 1960, and the first long trip to play all-nighters in Hamburg, that the band acquired the professionalism 'to play as if their lives depended on it'.[1] Their return to Liverpool, and in particular a live show in December 1960 which provided the first inklings of 'Beatlemania', saw them settled in as regulars at the city's Cavern Club to immense local enthusiasm. The record business, however, was not a provincial phenomenon, and it saw two further stints in Hamburg, in the springs of 1961 and 1962, and gigs all around north-west England before manager Brian Epstein, in a last-ditch effort, managed to secure an audition with George Martin, head of the tiny Parlophone label. The rest is well known, of course, but what may not be sufficiently appreciated is how different the Beatles appeared from their competitors in 1963. The cosmopolitan, street-hardened clientèle of the Hamburg clubs was not there to listen to the music: the rock 'n' roll material with which all members of the band had been infatuated since their school days of the mid-1950s, and which could be shouted and thrown about, was far more suitable to such an audience than the pop standards of the time. The constant playing of such material (itself frequently reworked) proved an incentive particularly to Lennon and McCartney to try their hand at making up songs. In British music at least, the division of labour between songwriter and performer had been virtually secure up to this point. The development of the Lennon–McCartney songwriting partnership, which gave rise to many others, can be seen as a taking of power by a new generation of performers.

The entry of rock 'n' roll material into British popular culture can be traced to two major sources, which will come to reflect the division in the later 1960s between 'rock' and 'pop'. Lonnie Donegan's place in Barber's band (see p. 4) was taken by Alexis Korner, who had far more interest in the 'blues' than 'jazz'. Korner and Barber brought over to the UK black US blues and rhythm 'n' blues singers such as Muddy Waters, Bill Broonzy, Sonny Terry and Brownie McGhee. These players were taken up by a number of art-college musicians, most specifically the Rolling Stones.[2] To a large extent, this development was confined to London. Liverpool's contribution owed more to its role as a major port of disembarkation from the USA. Sailors would bring home Fender guitars and the latest rock 'n' roll records which were unavailable in the UK. The Beatles' early style, then, grafted on to a skiffle base material from such diverse styles as rock 'n' roll (Chuck Berry, Fats Domino, Little Richard, Jerry Lee Lewis, Elvis Presley), rhythm 'n' blues (Bo Diddley, Smokey Robinson), rockabilly/country'n'western (Carl Perkins, Roy Orbison, Buddy Holly, the Everly Brothers) and even some mainstream pop (as sung by black girl groups such as the Chiffons).[3]

By the end of 1963, Beatlemania was at its height in the UK. Two albums (*Please Please Me* and *With the Beatles*) had already reached the top of the charts, while *A Hard Day's Night* and *Beatles For Sale* would match this success in 1964. The material throughout these albums was a mixture of Lennon–McCartney originals, staples from their live Hamburg sets, together with slices of rock 'n' roll/Motown and even the odd pop/country standard (such as 'A taste of honey').[4] At this time, it is the range of material, almost more than anything else, which sets the Beatles apart both from other Liverpool 'beat' bands and from bands in other parts of the country. Chambers calls attention to the easy coexistence in their early repertory of both *intensional* and *extensional* modes of construction, at least as far as the latter existed in Tin Pan Alley styles, arguing for a successful combination of the richness of Afro-American vocal articulation and an attention to harmonic and melodic construction.[5] The Beatles' music is thereby viewed as the offspring of a 'forbidden' exchange which was easily available through records, but which depended on the actual success of the Beatles for others to launch similar styles.

The Beatles' first American tour began in February 1964 (they had refused to go until they had a No. 1 single over there), as part of what has become known as the 'British invasion'. They had been immediately preceded by North London's Dave Clark Five, and were followed in close order by the London-based duos Peter and Gordon, and Chad and Jeremy, by London's Rolling Stones and Liverpool's Gerry and the Pacemakers. By 1965, bands as diverse as Manchester-based Herman's Hermits and the Newcastle-based Animals, and then London's the Who and Manchester's the Hollies, were added to the list.[6] Chart success is a reasonable indication of the importance of these 'British invasion' bands: there was only one UK success in the US charts in 1963, but in 1964 there were thirty-two. This period became crucial in the development of popular music. For the first time this century, British developments were exported to the USA; hitherto, in the USA, the idea of a British band had been faintly ridiculous. Through this route, Americans gradually encountered and accepted the return of their black heritage, but it was not a simple process. For whites, interest in black music was a pastime enjoyed only by an 'enlightened few' while, by mid-1960s, blacks had come to despise the blues and its accommodatory message in favour of soul and the Protestant ethic it embodied – not only 'things will improve' but 'I can help improve them'.[7] It did not take long, however, for this contribution to become devalued. John Gabree, for instance, arguing very soon after the appearance of *Sgt. Pepper*, insisted that the Beatles' importance was grossly overrated, and lumped them together with a band like Herman's Hermits (an avowedly 'pop' outfit bigger in the USA than the Beatles in 1965), against the counter-cultural force represented by Cream, Canned Heat and Frank Zappa's Mothers of Invention. Gabree decried the Beatles' politics as wishy-washy liberal, making it clear how difficult it had become to disentangle these worlds which, a couple of years earlier, had had nothing apparently in common.[8]

Perhaps this confusion began with Prime Minister Harold Wilson's politically convenient awarding of MBEs to the Beatles in 1964. Rock 'n' roll's demise had occurred more than five years before, as far as the media were concerned, to be replaced by a rejuvenated recourse to 'repetitive trivia' (Adam Faith, Billy Fury, Tommy Steele and Cliff Richard). This had purged the 'danger' from the Beatles' inheritance without dulling its unfamiliarity to the British mass audience. The birth of this popular music force coincided with the election which returned a Labour government for the first time in thirteen years, an election remembered today particularly for Wilson's campaign speech in which he spoke of the 'white heat of technological revolution'. Strangely, this era completed the change in capitalist emphasis from commodity production to the commercial and service sectors, expanding the working-class market for music of the 1950s into a middle-class youth market in the 1960s. Thus the maturation of the 'affluent' society, powered by Wilson's 'revolution'. Chambers argues that 'affluence' and 'modernization' were watchwords, suggesting the arrival of the classless society wherein everybody could be affluent. The roles of television, advertising and journalism in creating this myth are crucial, for the same media were implicated in the creation of the Beatles as a phenomenon. By 1966, far from being a marginalized pursuit, popular culture had become central, symbolized by the arrival of 'celebrities' (the media term was 'New Aristocrats') who, aside from secondary pursuits such as photography, modelling or commercial entrepreneurship, were primarily famous simply for being famous. And this was even to include bands like the Rolling Stones, uneasy in their assumption of aristocracy, whose celebrated bohemianism rather caused them to act as the marginalized 'other' to the untainted Fab Four.

'Swinging London' (and, in the popular media, Carnaby Street) was at the centre of this so-called classless society, as evidenced by contemporary accounts. For designer Gene Mahon (involved in the *Sgt. Pepper* cover) 'there were just so many scenes going on and you were part of one or another but they connected'. For 'New Aristocrat' (and greyhound trainer) Maldwyn Thomas, 'there were two things that everybody had in common: music and drugs. People grew up, came into pop music . . . and you just took the drugs and that sort of mingled everybody in and out of society. You got kids who used to live in the suburbs coming in and mixing with the Beatles.' Sue Miles, heavily involved in the birth of the underground *International Times*, suggests that the situation resulted from the affluence of the time, one with no big political issues, and a Labour government more progressive than the electorate; she cites issues such as homosexual and abortion law reform and the abolition of capital punishment. At the height of 'Swinging London' (1965), in an issue of *New Statesman*, Paul Johnson sounded an important but sour note: 'bewildered by a rapidly changing society, excessively fearful of becoming out of date, our leaders are increasingly turning to young people as guides and mentors – or, to vary the metaphor, as Geiger counters to guide them against the perils of mental obsolescence.' By now, we can see that the invention of youth as a separate culture, in the 1950s, has led to a position where society's only progressive values originate in that group. This is of course horribly complex and contradictory, for the more youth are trying to rebel, the more they are being coopted.[9]

Fashions changed with remarkable speed during the period immediately prior to 1967. In some respects, mod culture held sway (marked by the notion of 'affluence'), although it is difficult to clarify exactly what mod culture encompassed. For George Melly, the mods of 1963 represented the movement's 'second generation'; for the first generation, East End and South London 'discrete-hip' purists, clothes were all (this distinguished them from Teddy Boys), while the trad jazz revival was at its height. For Melly, a third phase became a catch-all for 'Swinging London' – this was 'mod' in the popular image. The mods' and rockers' battles of 1964 then involved the excessive neatness (an overblown adherence to Carnaby Street tastes) of this second generation. For Peter Wicke, writing from an East German perspective, mod not only meant the music of the Who, the Kinks, the Rolling Stones (!), the Small Faces, and the Spencer Davis Group, but also the Lambretta TV 175 (and no other model), fashionable suits, parkas, neat hair, and all-night dancing on speed (amphetamines). Mods were East End and South London working class, but other than that there was nothing special about them. Paul Weller (of the Jam and Style Council, and more recently a 'big name' solo artist) agrees with Wicke, citing the Carnaby Street phase as commercialization. Mods were 'clean, smart, working class, arrogant, anti-authoritarian with absolutely no respect for their elders', typified by the Who's Pete Townshend and the Small Faces' Steve Marriott. The 'purism' he espouses should probably, at this distance, be criticized as atavistic. Harry Shapiro focuses on 'Swinging London', but describes the earlier phase as 'too smart and too neat', i.e. as imbued with menace. The music of the mods was of no particular style, but it eventually focused on the Kinks and the Who. Shapiro insists that the Who's image was 'manufactured' – he talks of 'the desperate need to keep up appearances and stand behind the image'. He also refers to the Small Faces as mod's death-throes reincarnated as sanitized pop. Finally, in his crucial study, Stanley Cohen insists the Carnaby Street phase barely diluted the style of the original mods, while the refusal of the Stones and the Who to accommodate established behaviour reflected the mood of the Brighton, Clacton and Margate riots.[10]

During the course of 1967, mod culture was swept away by psychedelia (marked by the shift in drug use from amphetamines to LSD). The change is musically most obvious in the work of the Small Faces, but it can also be clearly seen in the pages of *New Musical Express*: prior to June 1967 and the release of *Sgt. Pepper* there were still many adverts for swinging and mod clothes (suits, turtle neck sweaters, etc.), but adverts for psychedelic clothing (tunics, bell-bottoms, capes) were in the ascendant by July. This is true for photos of artists too, particularly Jimi Hendrix, Cream, and the Herd (who are pictured in mod clothing but with a psychedelic slogan). The total geniality of this change is noted in MacDonald's insistence that English psychedelia (as opposed to its US counterpart) was not about love or drugs, but about the recovery of innocence.[11] This would have a profound effect upon *Sgt. Pepper*.

If there was no identifiable 'mod' style of music, even less was there a single identifiable 'pop' style between about 1963 and 1967. Key characteristics need to be assembled from diverse sources. The early style of the Beatles represented an amalgam of the range of largely black styles they were interested in emulating (soul, Motown, pop ballad, soul ballad, rock 'n' roll, rockabilly/country and western), but these were 'reorchestrated' for their own forces; the rich range of horns, pianos, organs, orchestral strings and the like (all of which are there either to fill out harmonies or to play melodic ideas) become transposed to the rhythm or, occasionally, lead guitar.[12] This instrumentation (lead, rhythm and bass guitars, kit, lead and backing vocals, but no keyboard instrument) was derived from skiffle via the Shadows and became the bedrock of British rock until the demise of the rhythm guitar with the birth of heavy rock (Jimi Hendrix, Eric Clapton). The amalgam emphasized a number of elements from rock 'n' roll and, ultimately, the blues – texture, melodic structure and pentatonicism, rhythm, and vocal style (impersonal and using responsorial textures) – combined with elements probably derived from Anglo-Celtic folk song – diatonic (and frequently modal, marked by the flattened seventh) melodies and verse-refrain

form – and elements from more advanced western harmony – orna-
mental chromaticisms together with triadic parallelism, ostinati and
modal progressions challenging any secure sense of key. This last is an
important point for, as Joan Peyser's contemporary discussion avers, the
Beatles and their contemporaries did not fight the war with dramatic
expressionism crucial to the generation at the beginning of the century, a
war in which *Pierrot Lunaire* represented an important skirmish. In
noting this range of characteristics, Richard Middleton insists that 'it is
the perpetual tempering of one element by another in such a cultural
mixture as this (as well as what is retained of the traditional blues techniques of objectification) which is responsible for the sense of irony and
control characteristic of the music'.[13]

Of the other artists cited by Shaw as constituent of the first wave of
the British invasion, only the Rolling Stones have been of lasting importance. Rather than having roots in rock 'n' roll and skiffle, the Rolling
Stones developed from trad jazz and rhythm 'n' blues. They were the
only band of their generation who were present at the formation of rock
and who had direct experience of the tours put together by Korner and
Barber. Muddy Waters had been brought over first in 1958, and his use of
electric guitar was perceived as a revelation. Brian Jones, founder
member of the Stones, had been present at Waters's first electric gig in
the Marquee, then in Central London's Oxford Street. When Alexis
Korner put together the band Blues Incorporated in 1961, his drummer
was Charlie Watts, who was subsequently a founder member of the
Stones. Watts was replaced in Korner's band by Ginger Baker (later of
Cream) when the former was reluctant to turn professional. The 'blues'
was always more deep-rooted in the Rolling Stones than it was in the
Beatles, even if it was not always prominent: Mick Jagger was reportedly
so enthusiastic he wrote to the Chess label to obtain records unobtainable
in England.[14] This degree of enthusiasm is similar to what was happen-
ing in Liverpool, except that Chess marketed rhythm 'n' blues rather
than rock 'n' roll.

From the middle of the 1960s, the Rolling Stones and the Beatles,
respectively, would come to symbolize one of the distinctions between
'rock' and 'pop'. In these terms, and being wary of the near-essentialism
involved, rock can be seen as extrovert, revolutionary and masculine,
whereas pop was more introvert, evolutionary and feminine.[15] This dis-

tinction was apparent in attitudes to interpersonal relationships (especially as expressed in songs): where rock was particularly self-centred ('I can't get no satisfaction'), pop created space for other-centredness ('She loves you'). The bluntness of this distinction is apparent – just think of Lennon's 'Run for your life'[16] – but it hides an important tendency. If the Beatles were appropriated as celebrators of affluence, the Rolling Stones were its 'other', its dark side. This was signified by Jagger's voice (the pout can literally be heard in the shape of the mouth as notes are chewed and expelled through protuberant lips), in the use of slide guitar (with a preponderance of mixolydian/aeolian riffs and few of the full diatonic melodies found in the Beatles), in the tone of their sentiments ('Paint it black'), in their daring subject matter (the misogynism of 'Under my thumb' or the glee of 'Mother's little helper') and in their brushes with the establishment (particularly the arrests for drug use).[17]

Neither the Beatles nor the Rolling Stones (*contra* Wicke) could be said to represent the music of the mods, who became the most important cultural grouping in the run-up to 1967. In the early years of the mods' 'final phase' (i.e. 1964–6), both the Kinks and the Who were thought representative, a mantle which had passed to the Small Faces by late 1966. Early influences on the Kinks' founder Ray Davies are remarkably similar to those we have already seen: bluesman Bill Broonzy, rock 'n' roller Chuck Berry, the Ventures (US forerunners of the Shadows), together with country guitarist Chet Atkins. Davies heard Korner in the early 1960s, and knew the newly formed Rolling Stones in 1962, although he made little use of the piano style R & B inherited from Little Richard or Fats Domino. The most important characteristic of the Kinks' early style distinguished it clearly from both the Beatles and the Stones: early songs like 'All day and all of the night' or 'Till the end of the day' (from 1964 and 1965) are based around a riff rather than a chord sequence.[18] The most immediate precursor of this technique was the Kingmen's 'Louie Louie', an American hit in 1963 (itself covered by the Kinks in 1965), although it can be traced back through 'jump' jazz (e.g. Louis Jordan's 'Saturday night fish fry') to swing (and even Glenn Miller's 'Pennsylvania 65000'). With the release of 'Dedicated follower of fashion' in the spring of 1966, the Kinks changed style to songs full of wry observation on contemporary life, a style that can be traced back through singers like Tommy Steele and ultimately to music hall. As George Melly observed: 'they stood aside watching, with sardonic amusement, the pop world chasing its own tail, and they turned out some of the most quirky intelligent grown-up and totally personal records in the history of British pop. Their ... strength ... was their ... refusal to join the club. They were ... hugely under-rated in consequence.'[19] Indeed, it is only very recently (i.e. 1995), with the rise of 'Britpop' and especially Blur, that Ray Davies's contribution is being re-evaluated. With the exception of some songs by the Beatles and, a decade later, Jam and Madness, this observational viewpoint has remained almost entirely untapped.

In their eschewal of a rhythm guitar in favour of a vocalist who could concentrate entirely on vocal projection, the Who seemed an attitudinally harder band from the outset. Leader Pete Townshend arrived on the scene too late to hear Muddy Waters, and so the black US influence was received second-hand. A song like 'Substitute' (1966), for example, manages a dense texture despite the sparse instrumentation, while the division of the verse into two parts is a distinctive structural precursor of heavy metal/hard rock. The change from two rhymes to four in these two parts of the verse seems to mark a loss of rhetorical expansiveness and an increase in verbally inexpressible anxiety that ultimately leads to violence. This controlled aggression is one thing that distinguished the mods, as does the structural neatness of a song like the Small Faces' 'All or nothing' (1966). 'All or nothing' is notable for its concern for textural shading. The verse is again in two parts, moving from picking guitar to power chord, and these are preceded by the even more delicate introduction. A more striking example occurs in the playout. A formulaic sequence is repeated a number of times at full volume, but includes a softer interpolation which intensifies the song's ultimate harmonic resolution. In contrast to the Beatles' Liverpool accent and falsetto, Jagger's pout or Daltrey's snarl, Steve Marriott generally used two distinct voices, the first a rich soul voice (reminiscent of Stevie Winwood and which would be further developed by Joe Cocker) and the second an authentic cockney, its discovery coinciding with Ray Davies's change of approach noted above. The use of an organ rather than a rhythm guitar strengthened the mods' links with soul (the organ was a particular staple for labels like Motown, Atlantic and Stax), while the strong mixolydian character of their harmonies suggests that few other bands had the Beatles' progressive (chromatic) harmonic outlook at the time.[20] By the time of the Small Faces' *Ogden's Nut Gone Flake* (late 1968), the whole recording was heavily phased, marking the change to psychedelia, which was mixed with ordinary reality in songs like 'Itchykoo Park'.[21] The most representative characteristics of mod music might be the structural neatness of the Small Faces or the controlled aggression of the Who, but problems arise trying to distinguish the Small Faces' neatness from the Beatles' ('Can't buy me love', for instance) or the Who's aggression from that of the Stones.

By the mid-1960s, 'popular' and its diminutive 'pop' were no longer synonymous. The latter now excluded the older generation of balladeers (Frank Sinatra, Tony Bennett, Andy Williams), although it probably did include British singers Engelbert Humperdinck (Gerry Dorsey) and Tom Jones. It also included all the groups, although those displaying any longevity (e.g. the Shadows) were already appealing more specifically to an older generation. Indeed, to a large extent, the distinction between (straight, square) 'popular' and (groovy, 'with it') 'pop' was crucial to the industry as it began to discover how to target its wider audience more precisely, and how to enable the subsequent incorporation of music as a branch of the leisure industry. This can be gleaned from the rise of radio stations. Although pop music was beamed from Europe by Radio Luxembourg, there was very little that would appear on the BBC. In 1964, Radio Caroline began broadcasting from a ship in the North Sea, grossing £750,000 in its first eighteen months. As an illegal operation they paid no royalties but received a healthy advertising revenue. Having banned such operations, the Labour government were forced to permit the BBC to set up its own version and Radio 1, its would-be rebellious offspring, was born late in 1967. It gradually became indistinguishable from its commercial competitors bar its lack of advertising (and, as some commentators would argue, its lack of quality). Pressure for franchises for commercial radio stations became unstoppable, however, leading to the current point where Radio 1 is just one of a number of (even national) players, constantly attempting to recoup listeners lost to more tightly marketed stations.[22] Such stations frequently appeal to advertisers' requirement for niche marketing, where marketing strategies for many goods are unthinkable without the right music to accompany them, a process which first became prominent in the UK in 1986 with Levi jeans' advert to Ben E. King's 'Stand by me' (1961).

Sgt. Pepper then, while popular, was not 'popular' but 'pop'. In retrospect, it was also possibly 'rock', as that generic term developed to account for the way the frivolous appeared to don the cloak of seriousness. How true that seriousness was will have to await discussion of the album itself.

3

Inception

There should have been nothing special about *Sgt. Pepper*.[1] April to June 1966 had seen the recording of the previous album *Revolver*, the Beatles' seventh successive UK No. 1, whose diverse and innovatory material and approach to production were to provide the impetus for journalists like *Melody Maker*'s Alan Walsh to bemoan the fact that pop music was growing up. In May 1967, prior to the release of *Sgt. Pepper*, Walsh was complaining that the Beatles (together with groups such as the Hollies and the Beach Boys) were losing contact with their fans through their growing reluctance to tour, to appear on television and to be interviewed.[2] Indeed, the autumn of 1966 had seen what was to be the Beatles' last tour, a decision that had been brewing for some time (due in large part to their inability even to hear themselves on stage because of the incessant adulation) and which was brought to a head by the nasty incident following their apparent failure to accord 'proper' respect to Imelda Marcos, wife of the Philippine dictator, on the Philippine leg of that tour.

In late November 1966, they began recording work on 'Strawberry Fields forever', which was intended to appear on the as-yet-unnamed eighth British album.[3] In one sense, this was to mark a new departure. Having decided not to tour any more, the Beatles' entire musical effort could be devoted to the studio. While they clearly perceived this as a release, it necessarily created its own pressures in that their studio work would have to become valid in its own right, rather than function as an adjunct to other activities. This is not a simple issue, since the decision to stop touring was both caused by, and the cause of, the decision to become a 'studio band'. The context for this new departure was broad. The Beach Boys' *Pet Sounds* (Brian Wilson's response to the Beatles' earlier *Rubber Soul*) had received intense critical acclaim (the band were advertised as the 'World's no.1 group' in *New Musical Express* of 29 April 1967), and McCartney particularly felt the need to go one better; William Mann's influential *Times* review describes the rather stagnant pool populated by the Monkees, protest music, the vaudeville revival, beat music and 'sticky, sweaty, vacuous' ballads; and years before the supposed incorporation of 'Baroque', 'Classical' and 'Indian' techniques within progressive rock (see chapter 6), Bob Dawbarn was complaining of their intrusion in mid-1967.[4]

In a second sense, it was business as usual, since this was merely another album. Brian Epstein and George Martin's 'master plan' of two albums (and four singles) a year had begun to slip, and a new album soon was necessary in order to keep the band in public view. At this stage, Lennon and McCartney were toying with the notion of taking as a theme (itself a novel idea) the exploration of childhood sites and memories in Liverpool. 'Strawberry Field' was, in fact, a children's home in whose woods Lennon used to play.[5] December and January had seen the recording of two further songs on this theme: 'When I'm sixty-four' (actually written by Paul some years earlier, for his beloved father) and 'Penny Lane', a genuine locale whose street scene is partly of McCartney's invention. January 19 saw the first attempt at 'A day in the life'. McCartney's 'interlude' ('Woke up, fell out of bed . . .'), which was not inserted into the song until the following day, was built out of schoolday reminiscences, but Lennon's original verses simply retold three events: newspaper accounts of a survey of road holes in Blackburn and of the death of aristocrat Tara Browne, and Lennon's part the previous year in the film *How I Won the War*. The celebrated orchestral crescendi (beginning at $1'40''$ and $3'46''$) appear to have been McCartney's conception, apparently the result of being influenced by 'avant-garde' composers, particularly Stockhausen. Indeed, in his early review, Wilfrid Mellers found echoes of Stockhausen's *Momente* in the album's incorporated audience 'applause and laughter off'.[6] At about this point, it appears that the theme of exploring childhood began to vanish. In any event, 'Strawberry Fields forever' and 'Penny Lane' were released in February as a single, at the demand of Parlophone's US partner, Capitol.

It was not until 1 February, and the first takes of 'Sgt. Pepper's Lonely Hearts Club Band', that McCartney realized the potential for creating a live show out of this fictitious persona, which could be inhabited by the

Beatles themselves. The strange mixture of an Edwardian brass band transported to psychedelic San Francisco (and whose name was suggested to McCartney by those of various West Coast bands such as Jefferson Airplane and Quicksilver Messenger Service) itself rather typifies the age. George Martin notes that the military turn which this was given, particularly on the album cover, was partly a send-up of the US in Vietnam.[7] We should not, however, read too much into a professed counter-cultural stance at this stage. The hippies' political 'programme' (if that is not too coherent a concept) was more deeply founded on the celebration of diversity, a celebration intrinsic to two primary cultural sources, the Hindu (model for British hippies in the wake of the Maharishi Mahesh Yogi) and the Amerind (model for US hippies). This diversity found ready expression in the non-contradictory sporting of both kaftans and military uniforms (by the Beatles among others).

The following week saw the first takes of 'Good morning good morning' and 'Fixing a hole', and any authentic historical location for Sgt. Pepper's band vanishes together with them. Lennon's 'Good morning good morning' seems to have taken its inspiration from his addiction to television (which was frequently on as background while he was writing), in particular a Kellogg's Corn Flake advert (the crowing cock) and the contemporary situation comedy 'Meet the Wife'. McCartney's 'Fixing a hole' developed out of do-it-yourself exploits at his newly acquired derelict farmhouse in Campbeltown on the Kintyre peninsula in Scotland. At least, that is the official (i.e. McCartney's own) account. In tune with the times, however, the belief that the 'hole' to be 'fixed' was in McCartney's arm (i.e. with heroin) was widespread. Indeed, the album's only line which appears to have been intentionally provocative was 'I'd love to turn you on', from 'A day in the life'. Even here, though, McCartney claimed that they were trying to turn people on to the 'truth' rather than drugs, despite their own heavy usage of LSD and marijuana during this period.

February also saw the first takes of four more songs. Harrison's 'It's only a northern song' was jettisoned from the project within days, while 'Being for the benefit of Mr Kite', 'Lovely Rita' and 'Lucy in the sky with diamonds' were further distanced from any Sgt. Pepper persona. The lyrics for Lennon's 'Mr Kite' were taken almost wholesale from a Victorian circus poster bought by him a matter of days previously.

Lennon's own views on the song's quality swung at different times from it being a 'throwaway' to its 'purity'. The description of the doughty Rita as a 'meter maid' was derived from an American friend of McCartney's, while the title of Lennon's 'Lucy in the sky with diamonds' was taken from a school painting by son Julian (aged four at the time). Much of the imagery in this derives from Lennon's love of the Goons (Peter Sellers, Spike Milligan, Harry Secombe) and Lewis Carroll: in interview McCartney suggested that for Lennon 'Lucy was God, the big figure, the White Rabbit', although MacDonald argues that she was the '"lover/mother" of his most helpless fantasies'.[8] The painting is reproduced in Turner's study. The acronymic reference to lysergic acid was apparently not initially intended by Lennon: the debate it spawned will be discussed in chapter 5. In each of these songs, we can see that the concern while writing is neither to know what the song is about, nor to recount a narrative or relate a message, but merely to work. A casual phrase or encounter will set off an idea which is then worked on, according to its own logic, but without the slightest care for any prospective audience. This is not to say that the Beatles were averse to preaching, of course, or to addressing intimate relationships, but it is a mistake to attempt to find a definitive message hidden within every set of lyrics. (This has caused problems for many commentators, though not necessarily for fans. I shall return to the issue in chapter 5.)

This refusal to preach is not the case with 'Within you without you', George Harrison's accepted contribution to the project, and the second of four songs which began recording during March. In 1965, Harrison had become interested in the congruence between LSD-induced loss of ego and that espoused by Hindu sects, and this was the first of many attempts to 'return from the mountain to the market-place'.[9] Although both Lennon and McCartney showed passing interest in 1967-8, and though all later admitted disillusion with the person of the Maharishi, Harrison's conversion had real substance, as reflected in his view of the audience. Responding to a journalist's question, 'having achieved world-wide fame by singing pleasant, hummable numbers don't they feel they may be too far ahead of the record-buyers?'; George thinks not: 'People are very, very aware of what's going on around them nowadays. They think for themselves and I don't think we can ever be accused of under-estimating the intelligence of our fans.'[10] 'Getting better' was another song sparked off by an odd phrase, in this case the title. In a conversation between McCartney and biographer Hunter Davies, McCartney acknowledged that it had been the only comment they could ever get out of Jimmy Nicol, stand-in drummer for a week of touring in 1964. 'She's leaving home' was taken from a newspaper article, although a few of the details, and the protagonists' motivations, were supplied by McCartney.

So, by mid-March, songs were being written in great haste in order to fulfil the requirements of the album. According to Davies, this was usual procedure for the Beatles. The early songs written for an album might well have developed from a lot of inspiration and rewriting, but towards the end it became 'simply' a hack job. Indeed, Davies's illustration, 'Being for the benefit of Mr Kite', was certainly not one of the last to be written, so we may assume that the practice of writing 'on the hop' accounts for a large proportion of the album.[11]

While the reprise of 'Sgt. Pepper's Lonely Hearts Club Band' (a suggestion of roadie Neil Aspinall) would be recorded on 1 April, the last full song to emerge from the recording studio was 'With a little help from my friends'. It was written specifically for Ringo to sing (it was usual for him to have one track per album). With the characteristically Liverpudlian persona of 'Billy Shears', the song created the opportunity to reinforce the 'live show' illusion of the album. This illusion seems to have been intended without any irony, and certainly seems to have deceived a few early critics.[12] Hunter Davies's 1968 biography gives an interesting description of the genesis of this song. His piece sounds like an eye-witness account but, although an active observer throughout the period, he is careful not to claim it as such. In any event, he describes a process wherein Lennon and McCartney worked together on the song, without a clear idea of where it was to go, or what it would be about – they began with nothing but the opening line, and simply repeated musical phrases over and over at the guitar or piano, throwing possible lines, and even single words, back and forth. Clearly, what was always of primary importance was the way it sounded, with precise meaning rather secondary. This process continued even in the company of a disinterested audience: friend Terry Doran (the 'man from the motor trade' of 'She's leaving home') and Lennon's wife, Cynthia. Composing was frequently interrupted by excursions into different songs (both their own and those of others), jokes and snack breaks. 'With a little help from my friends' seems to have fallen into place on their return from one of the latter, as if their combined subconscious faculties had been working on it in the mean time. The final verse of the song was written in the studio in this way immediately prior to recording the first takes (a not unusual procedure for the band since the label's ownership of the studio greatly lowered costs through avoiding rehearsal and recording studio fees). This, in large part, was the special strength of the Lennon–McCartney songwriting partnership. Although a particular song may have been principally the work of one writer (unlike this example), the other frequently contributed the most telling word or phrase which could turn it around (e.g. Lennon's 'it can't get much worse' in 'Getting better'). It is no exaggeration to claim that, on the dissolution of the songwriting partnership, neither writer alone was able to reproduce the strength of interaction (as McCartney may presciently have observed in *Abbey Road*'s 'Carry that weight').

The speed of work, then, was impressive. So much so that before the end of April (the album was not released until 1 June) the Beatles were again in the studio recording the title song to the film *Magical Mystery Tour*, a concept which had only come to McCartney on a flight a fortnight earlier. They were not even involved in the stereo mixes for *Sgt. Pepper*. Stereo was still a new development, and although all their songs were mixed in mono with great attention, the band were happy to allow George Martin free rein with the stereo mix. This did not create as much leeway as it might sound: in mixing from only four tracks, there is often little choice as to where to place and balance particular sounds. Even the running order seems to have been left up to Martin with the Beatles giving final approval, although they had played around with possible orders. Martin's lengthy rationale for the running order makes it clear that 'Side One' generally carried greater weight than 'Side Two' (many listeners would only listen to side one of an album, switching to another album rather than listen to side two), while the placing last of 'A day in the life' was purely pragmatic: nothing could possibly follow its greatly extended piano fade.[13]

As I suggested, then, there should have been nothing special about *Sgt. Pepper*. Accounts of its genesis and architecture paint it as something of a mixed bag. It was not the 'all-time killer album' planned in meticulous detail from beginning to end. As Martin points out, the

Beatles sensed a strong challenge from the Beach Boys' album *Pet Sounds* (and also the single 'Good vibrations' of 1966), both in terms of production values and songwriting, but such concerns were not evident in the manner in which *Sgt. Pepper* was put together. Contemporary media reports imply the Beatles were trying to keep their heads above the waves not only of the Beach Boys, but also of the Monkees, Jimi Hendrix, Dave Dee, Spencer Davis, Procol Harum, to name but the most prominent. The Beatles had been virtually incommunicado for months; more significantly, *Sgt. Pepper* was an album put together almost out of control, and, as such, it encapsulated the group's career, despite the efforts of Epstein, Martin, even McCartney. George Martin was to write nearly three decades later: 'By 1966 the Beatles were in a car that was going downhill very fast. This is not to say that their career was going downhill; but they were a media juggernaut that was increasingly out of their manager Brian Epstein's control – and everybody else's, for that matter. It wasn't so much that somebody was pressing the accelerator too hard; it was that nobody had their foot on the brake.'[14]

4

Commentary

The recording studio is an invigorating place in which to work. Pressures of time and competing personalities can forge the most stimulating aural experiences from piecemeal, often banal, structures. In the case of *Sgt. Pepper*, such pressures have bequeathed us an album of thirteen discrete songs, marketed in a sleeve which conveys the illusion of a coherent package (rather than a 'mixed bag'), wherein the order of the songs (notwithstanding today's CD technology) is highly important. In this chapter, I shall consider each song in turn and conclude with some brief remarks on the entire set and on that packaging, asking how the incoherent strands of material reported in chapter 3 were projected on to an assumed audience. We already have gutsy, impressionistic accounts in plenty – most rock journalists have offered us their interpretations at one time or other – but they tend to tell us more about the writer than the song. I shall represent myself as offering an 'objective' account of what each song is, counterpointing my interpretations with those of specific others where the differences are significant. My guiding principle has been that the visceral pleasures, those pleasures beyond the reach of discussion or analysis which these songs offer, are not the only ones, nor are they ultimately the most significant.[1]

Writing in 1996, two crucial issues impinge on the way the texts of popular music need to be approached. On the one hand, it is no longer widely accepted that the 'meaning' of a text is immanent in that text – rather, the meaning is 'socially constructed' among its listeners. This body of listeners cannot be reduced to holding a single view or even a coherent spread of views. On the other hand, it is hard to know what meaning a text might take on, without first knowing what that text might be: a possible approach is to note that texts *afford* a range of meanings (particularly where the text is under-coded),[2] without specifying what they must be in some sort of transcendent manner. Some writers would lump together the constructions of the text itself as entirely socially determined, in the same way that 'scientific' facts have recently been challenged as wholly constructed (a dogmatic position recently demolished by Alan Chalmers).[3] In any case, in this chapter I veer between consideration of what actually constitutes the text, and suggestions as to what it might mean. In doing so, some use will be made of rudimentary analytical sketches. The attentive reader will notice that much of my graphic vocabulary is borrowed from Schenkerian analysis. The diagrams are not, however, intended to function as Schenkerian analyses of these songs: I have discussed elsewhere my unease at the growing tendency to treat popular music as the linear continuation of classical tonality. Here, I appropriate some thoughts from Allen Forte's recent reorientation of Schenkerian methods to accommodate popular music, in particular his refusal to divine an *Ursatz* for the repertory he discusses.[4] Readers should note that the inner parts of these diagrams do not qualify as transcriptions; their only function is to enable identification of the harmony. In such a guitar-based style, inner parts (especially) do not obey any conventional voice-leading rules.

Sgt. Pepper's Lonely Hearts Club Band. 95 bpm; 1'58".

Presentations of ambiguity are crucial to this first song. The album opens with 10" of instrumental tuning and audience noises and, immediately, the listener is placed within a public environment. In what may have been intended as a joke, the instruments we hear tuning are orchestral strings, rather than the brass instruments of Sgt. Pepper's band. This environment remains throughout, although at 1'47" the continuity of audience applause is interrupted. It sounds as if the clip (from Martin's recording of the Cook/Moore/Bennett/Miller satire *Beyond the Fringe*) has been spliced together. The song is strangely structured, being a symmetrical arrangement of two separate strains. Twelve bars[5] (made up of a four-bar instrumental introduction and eight-bar 'verse' beginning at 22") give way to a five-bar brass interlude. A central twelve-bar section (56"– 1'26") halves the speed of melodic motion (i.e. from semiquavers to quavers) and leads to a repeat of the five-bar section before a final twelve bars: eight for the 'verse' (beginning at 1'38"), two bars of brass and two on 'Billy', which will resolve at 'Shears' (1'58") on to the key chord of the second song. This is summarized in Figure 4.1.

Bar lengths: 12 (4+8) + 5 + 12 + 5 + 12 (8+(2+2))

Beginning at: 12" 43" 56" 1'26" 1'38"

Fig. 4.1

This arrangement points, perhaps, to the song's underlying subtlety and range. Note the mixture of long-term rhymes ('years' in verse 1 with 'Shears' in verse 3) and their lack (in the second five-bar segment from 1'26": 'here'/'thrill'/'audience'/'with us'). These two distinct segments are further differentiated, but are also neatly linked. The song is in G mixolydian: in the opening and closing sections, G and its subdominant are linked by A; in the central section, they are linked by B♭. These chords can be interpreted as mutually exclusive, being members of alternative fifth-cyclic patterns (B♭–F–C–G–D and F–C–G–D–A), although modal patterns based on both I–II–IV and I–III–IV are equally common in rock.[6] This fourth-bounded segment of the pentatonic scale is also used motivically. Example 4.1 identifies some such instances (motif 'a'). The voices are rather idiosyncratically placed within the stereo image: Paul McCartney's best 'Little Richard' holler[7] to the far right in the outer sections (along with the opening guitar solo); three-part harmony to the left in the central section, where it supplies continuity to the rather energetic offbeat kit attacks; and finally unison voices to the centre over the second brass interlude, dramatizing the point of stylistic fusion.

Mellers considers this ambiguity to indicate that 'this public show-piece hides beneath its zest a certain jitteriness', although his insistence on harmonic false relations is a little out of place – the B♭ acts much more as a stylistically apt blue third than as a counter to the tonic's major third. For MacDonald, this ambiguity pits unsubtle three-chord heavy rock (unsubtle, because of the lack of a rhythm guitar) in the opening and closing sections against Edwardian period fashion in the five-bar interludes, fusing them in the central section as I have demonstrated. For Middleton, the mixture of mainstream and pop will come to symbolize both the collapse of the old social solidarity and the as yet inchoate new tribal solidarity.[8]

Ex. 4.1

For an 'overture', the song expresses a surprising modesty, which perhaps hides a hint of magic, in that the band were taught in a single day. It is taken only at a medium speed, contains deprecatory admissions in the band being 'out of style' and their moderate ability to 'raise a smile'

and employs only a very limited range. In the outer sections ($22''$–$43''$ and from $1'\,38''$), this extends to a 'blue third' above G, but the melody remains static. In the central section (from $56''$), the melody extends to a fourth below G. This also reverses the first section's upward tendency with the downward scale (in the brass), itself giving rise to motif 'b' in the central section (the direct reversal of the first section's melodic profile – again see Ex. 4.1). The first brass interlude approaches a structural G from below without achieving it, a process intensified in the central section and again in the vocal version of the interlude, such that the arrival on G at $1'38''$ feels exhaustively prepared, supporting the stylistic fusion mentioned above. Thus, the song neatly balances the processual and the architectural (the 12–5–12–5–12 bar layout).

With a little help from my friends. 116 bpm; 2′43″.

This song leads directly out of the first (the disc jockey's beloved 'segue'), strongly contributing to the illusion of the coherent package by virtue of its continuity. It has a standard format: two verses/refrains followed by a bridge (what is often called a 'middle eight', although it is frequently not of eight bars' length); a third verse/refrain and bridge; and a final (altered) refrain. The melodic range is limited to five notes for the most part (to suit Ringo Starr's voice) but, aside from this practical restriction, subtleties abound. The beat is solid, but Ringo frequently changes articulation (the 'groove'): to a hi-hat foundation ($9''$) he adds snare ($18''$), loses the force of the shuffle pattern ($26''$), reintroduces it ($43''$) after the wonderfully judged cymbal-less two-bar break, adds resonance on the hi-hat ($50''$), thickens the groove with a tambourine ($1'01''$), kills it ($1'26''$) but adds ride cymbal ($1'31''$) (etc.). These give the lie to Clayson's jibe that Ringo's role in the album was simply 'like being a session musician', even if others controlled where he came in.[9]

The song alternates the verse's uncertainty (what Middleton sees as the vulnerability of the teenager) with the refrain's security (Middleton's necessity of solidarity to which the opening song referred). This distinction is underpinned by harmony and vocal contour. The 'uncertain' verse uses a 'more tense', sharp-side harmonic pattern (E–B–f♯) whose melody resolutely remains around the note G♯, whereas the refrain uses the 'more relaxed', mixolydian flat-side D–A–E, with a

Ex. 4.2

melody slipping down to E. This relaxation is intensified by the final C–a^6–E cadence. The general sense of the verse's melody is one of stasis (beginning and ending on the same pitch, containing very limited scalic movement), but this hides a structural descent of a third (G♯ →E, or B →G♯) articulated by upward thirds (G♯ →B, F♯ →A, E →G♯) (see Ex. 4.2). Having recovered the verse's zenith pitch (B), the refrain is released to sink to the tonic. This process is subtle for, in the first verse and after the 'Billy Shears' introduction which rises to G♯, we are encouraged to hear the G♯→E motion as primary. In the third verse, however, after the intervening upper E→C♯ motion, we are encouraged to hear B→G♯ as primary, with the refrain finally sinking to E. This third verse, of course, features a reversal of position, with Ringo responding to his colleagues' queries, and seeming to achieve security through gaining a measure of control. Further subtleties include the richness of McCartney's bass lines: the verse's E–B–f♯–B–E sequence is played in three different ways. Starr's persona is crucial to the song: Mellers regards him as the least articulate band member and thus, as MacDonald notes, the song appears both communal (he is the fans' representative in the band) and personal (as Riley insists, he is singing about himself to both the audience and the band). He is placed fractionally to the left in the stereo image, balanced by the bass fractionally to the right (a technique which would become widespread by the turn of the decade), while the constant backing supports him dead centre. Other forces (tambourine and cymbal, guitar, backing voices, piano) surround him at various points, but without destroying his underlying stability. Indeed, on the final reiterations of the title, he seems to have merged with those backing voices.

Lucy in the sky with diamonds. 46 bpm; 3′26″.

Structurally, 'Lucy' is not problematic, consisting as it does of a double-strain verse and a refrain, thus: verse 1, refrain, verse 2, refrain, first strain, refrain repeated to fade. The verse and refrain are distinguished by their tempi: the first verse is in a slow 12/8 (four triplet beats to the bar) at 46 bpm, while the refrain doubles the tempo (to 93 bpm) but replaces triplets with straight beats. This 'metric modulation' is not easy to execute, and as a result the tempi of the second and third verses wander slightly (51 bpm and 49 bpm). On the cut recently released on the album *Anthology 2*, the shift is executed with slightly more security. The temporal shift is matched by ambiguous tonics: the verse moves from A (accompanied by a chromatically descending bass) to B♭, reaching G for the refrain, at the end of which V is reinterpreted as IV of A for the next verse. This is summarized in fig. 4.2.

```
||: A A⁷ D d :||... B♭ C F B♭ C G D ||: G C D:|| D
A:  I    IV          B♭: I II V I II                    A: IV→I
                          G: IV I V      I IV V
    6″                        32″        42″        50″  1′06″
```

Fig. 4.2

At the end of the song, this reinterpretation fails to take place, but neither does the melody resolve to a low G, despite the fact that melodic lines descend (through only a fourth or fifth during the verses) throughout. Indeed, structurally important pitches fall from D (at 32″) to A, to the absent G (which is replaced by its upper octave) and finally to a struc-

Ex. 4.3

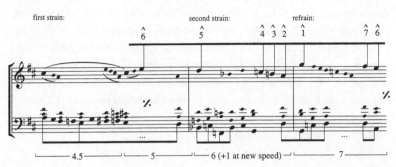

(becomes 8 on final repeats)

tural E implied in the first part of subsequent verses – it is the very model of illusory movement (see Ex. 4.3). The surface descents (e.g. opening C♯–B–A) are complemented, although four times as slowly, by those of the bass. They were a very late discovery, for the guide vocal for the track (released on *Anthology 2*) remains for far longer on C♯. The frequently asserted LSD references in the song are supported by 'abnormalities' in texture and production: the drifting of the double-tracked voice (e.g. 24″–27″); the Indian tambura (18″–, 1′10″–); the phasing on the bass (*c.* 1′40″); what sounds like a Leslie speaker through which the guitar is played (*c.* 52″);[10] and, perhaps most notably, the general avoidance of a drum beat in the verses' first strains (notable for the emptiness of their texture), which allows a sense of impressions simply to waft in. Even where the kit does come in strongly, in the refrain, Starr's characteristic loose-skinned tom-toms and dull snare add to the effect.

As we have seen, the acronymic reference to 'LSD' seems to have been (at least initially) unintended; response to its presence has been predictably mixed. Derek Jewell saw the song as 'splendid [almost metaphysical] urban poetry', while Jack Kroll focused on its 'Sitwellian images'. Mellers suggests the song makes more sense as a 'revocation of the dream-world of childhood' than as an LSD song (he notes that 'Lucy' comes from the Latin for 'light'!), while Riley sees it as 'artful happenstance of child's play'. This view is disliked by Goldstein, who argues that in this song 'tone overtakes meaning' (a view I have already criticized), while the song is, not surprisingly, crucial to Whiteley's interpretation of the entire album as drug-related. Both these possible interpretations (childhood/LSD) are encompassed by Middleton, who sees the song as a taking of refuge in hallucination, while remaining equivocal about its validity, an equivocation perhaps best sited in the 'clod-hopping' refrain, with its markedly different harmonies and tempo. Indeed, MacDonald charges Lennon with excessive pliancy in the face of McCartney's bass and counter-melody, a pliancy itself probably the result of LSD indulgence, while Goldstein bemoans Lennon's exchange of raunchiness for mere caprice (throughout the album), perhaps due to the same cause.[11]

Getting better. 118 bpm → 126 bpm @ 45″; 2′47″.

This song's structure is a little more complex, involving incremental growth, as shown in Figure 4.3.

Introduction	2 bars	
Verse 1	(4 + 4) bars,	melodic structure A B B′ A
Refrain	((4 + 4) + 2),	melodic structure C C
Verse 2	(4 + 4)	
Refrain	((4 + 4) + 2) + (2 + (4 + 4))	
Verse 3	(5 + 4)	
Refrain	((4 + 4) + 2) + (2 + (4 + 4)) + 6 to fade	

Fig. 4.3

This expansion, which takes place separately across verses and refrains, perhaps underscores the progressive ('getting better'), 'ebullient'[12] nature of the lyrics and can be sensed in the articulation of the verses, from Lennon's blue third interjections in verse 1, through the thickening of the vocal line in thirds in verse 2, to the expanded confession of verse 3. The song is harmonically straightforward, being based on I, IV and V in C with deceptively simple incursions through II and III (e.g. from 28″–32″), all hung beneath an insistent high G pedal on guitar which is dominant from the outset, occurring as it does over IV. The pitch G is also crucial in the bass (with its upward octave leaps) and the melody, with top G acting as the song's goal. It is briefly touched via an arpeggiation of V but is lost in the outer ('A') lines of the verse (10″ – 'mad', 22″ – 'up'), it is reached for again at the beginning of the verse

Ex. 4.4

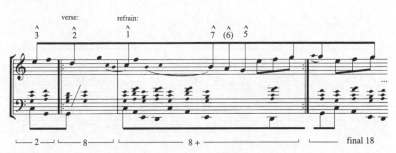

(27″ and 35″ – 'better') and finally attained from below in the last line of
the refrain (39″ and 1′14″ – 'been') and from above in the second refrain
(1′16″ – 'getting') via an arpeggiation of I. This sense of achievement is
reached despite the general stasis of the melody (which tends to focus
only on D and C in turn). As Example 4.4 shows, however, the general
downward motion of structural pitches allows the attainment of G at the
end of the refrain to be strengthened by the achievement of its lower
octave in the immediately preceding bar.

Riley interprets 'Getting better' as a refreshing but silly love song, and
Mellers sees it similarly, suggesting that the song's 'perky insouciance'
prevents us from taking the first verse's denunciation ('can't complain'),
and the third verse's confession (the casual abuse which confirmed that
'all you need' was far more than simply 'love'), very seriously. These
views are, perhaps, belied by the song's careful construction. For
Middleton, these difficulties are in fact resolved in the refrain through
love, perhaps at the point where the dogged bass drone of the verse gives
way to the light treble drone. Percussion articulation is again very neat,
moving from the hi-hat fourth-beat anticipations of the outer verses to
the second-beat handclaps of the second verse, to the conga playout. It
also contains one of those moments of very neat production which made
George Martin so crucial to the partnership. Following the wonderful
rhythmic lightness of the passage from 1′36″, and the entry of the percussion at 1′48″ (with Starr's excellently judged offbeat cymbal), at 1′57″
the departure of the tambura drone is covered by the entry of a low piano,
well masking the change of ambiance (although even Martin could not
excise the counting-in during the two introductory bars).

Ex. 4.5

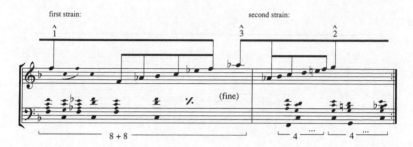

Fixing a hole. 110 bpm → 114 bpm @ 1'50"; 2'35".

This song is simpler still, making use of a two-strain verse which extends to sixteen and eight bars respectively. The first strain of verse 2 substitutes an eight-bar instrumental for its second half, and the first (and only) strain of verse 3 extends to twenty-four bars and beyond into the fade. The song is based squarely on F, shifting a little to the flat-side in the first strain (C^7, f^7 and $B\flat^9$ harmonies result this time from a chromatic inner part) and to the sharp-side (C, G and D) in the second. These leanings are reflected in the melody: although the thrust is upwards throughout, the scale of the first strain tends to be pentatonic, while in the second strain it is diatonic, reaching a G which resolves back to the tonic F at the beginning of each first strain, or alternatively reaches up to topmost A♭ at the end of the song. The uncomplicated tenor of the lyrics finds ready expression in a structure which seems to maintain the pitches F and C unchallenged throughout (see Ex. 4.5).

Instrumental parts are again carefully thought out: although the generally static bass may appear to root McCartney's wandering mind, it still manages many changes of articulation (for example in the first strain of verse 2), as does the kit (note its increased presence at 25") and the introduction of backing vocals at 1'33". We have already seen this with other songs (the changes during the very first strain are particularly noticeable). The wandering is clearly pleasurable: note how McCartney's articulation seems to issue from an open smile, together with his subtle wandering from the beat, as he describes the 'colourful way'. Care is also apparent in the guitar break in verse 2 which, rather than heading ever higher (as was becoming customary in recordings from 1966–7), neatly sinks to the bottom register of the instrument (MacDonald finds it distracted and introverted). This is mixed to the extreme right, with the voice and bass central and the kit and harpsichord to the left, meaning that the first verse sounds a little unbalanced. The entry of backing voices towards the end, also to the right, suggests that the 'hole' is now completely filled.

As with a number of these songs, the contrast between the two strains permits Riley's interpretation, in which the song's emotional ambiguity is couched in musical equivocation as the song fades with its minor/flat-wise, 'open' pattern. Mellers relates the wandering mind to a search for identity while, in the context of the whole, Middleton views the song as a proposed solution (to the problem posed at the outset) but an unsatisfactory, because solipsistic, one.

She's leaving home. 128 bpm; 3′33″.

This is the first song on the album not to use the group's guitars and drums: here we have a string nonet plus harp. This alone causes parallels to be made with the earlier 'Yesterday' (string quartet) and 'Eleanor Rigby' (octet), although Goldstein's negative review finds this song uninspired. He insists that it sounds like an immense put-on in comparison to 'Eleanor Rigby', being typical of McCartney's 'Pop magnificats' which have by now become 'merely politely profound'. MacDonald, on the other hand, calls 'She's leaving home' one of the two best songs on the album. Opposing criteria are clearly at work: Goldstein (in 1967) is celebrating the burgeoning counter-culture and MacDonald (in 1995) is intensely aware of its failings.

The song alternates thirty-two-bar (four-strain) verses with nineteen-bar refrains (made up of 8 + 4 + 7), except that the final verse is only sixteen bars in length, and the final refrain stretches to 12 + 16, giving an air of completion that is supported by the novel plagal cadence. The harmonic sequence is based on a simple cycle of fifths from the tonic E, slipping to D, and then to c♯ (11″ or 1′23″ etc.), to F♯/f♯, to B (17″ or 1′29″) and back to E (28″ or 1′44″ etc.). The positive sense of direction given by this harmonic sequence is counteracted in a number of ways. Twice, the syllable 'down' (28″, 1′41″) is emphasized in a manner that makes the listener's stomach drop – the note and the silence immediately preceding it

Ex. 4.6

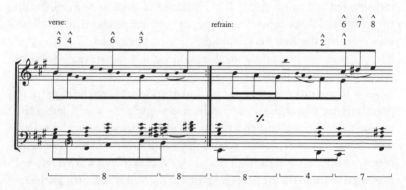

are comparatively long, and for the only time in the song we have an upbeat: 'she goes/she breaks'. It is as if the experiencing body is only now beginning to appreciate the crisis. McCartney's apparent emotion has been heard previously (particularly the deep, and nearly inaudible, sigh at 14″), while his audible temptations to syncopation are rigidly held in check. The surface vocal contour continually falls, until the strong harmonic support offered by c♯ and B permit a slight rise. Yet the lower E is only reached at the end, over a chord of c♯, with Lennon's faintly sneering 'bye-bye' (and with Lennon slightly flat at this point and McCartney sharp on his preceding high E, the failure of communication is neatly dramatized). Even in the coda, where this 'bye-bye' is reharmonized, it resolves over IV, leaving the final I for strings and harp alone. As if to confirm this near failure, upper Es in the melody never coincide with harmonies of E. This perhaps points to the melodic structure which moves in both directions from the opening B to both lower and upper E, as in Example 4.6. Note that both the initial $\hat{5}$–$\hat{3}$ and subsequent $\hat{3}$–$\hat{1}$ movements are underpinned by a harmonic I–VII–VI sequence, while $\hat{5}$–$\hat{6}$ patterns are constantly reharmonized. The song seems less a celebration of a generation gap than a narrative of inter-personal disaster and daring compassion in its telling. This is an interpretation Walter Everett[13] finds symbolized in the music, where both the actual and metaphorical distance of daughter from home are symbolized by the growth of a single motif. The cello line at 13″ acquires a contrary violin line at 35″ which, after alternative articulations in verse 2, adds pandiatonic upper voices at 2′38″. This underlies what he describes as the song's homology of affect and lyrical interpretation.

'She's leaving home' is clearly more full of sentiment than the rather dispassionate 'Eleanor Rigby'. This is due in large part to Mike Leander's orchestration: Martin was unlikely to have fallen for such clichés as the string tremolos to support the girl's fluttering excitement as she waits to keep her appointment. In contrast to Goldstein, Mac-Donald finds the sentiment apt, for reconciliation is possible, although it did not take place for the protagonists of the original situation. Mellers reads the continual F♯ → B moves in the verse's second and fourth strains as frustrated modulations to B, and lays great stress on the melody of the opening eight bars (for instance) subdividing into five bars of voice answered by three of cello. He suggests that this irregularity of structure *enacts* the story, in that it represents a failure all round, from both generations. While this seems to me to be going too far, reading into the structure of a late twentieth-century song characteristics expected in late eighteenth-century Vienna,[14] the gentleness of Lennon's interjections (that the parents were unaware of their failure until too late, and that the daughter was unable properly to communicate her feelings even in print) supports Mellers's interpretation.

Being for the benefit of Mr Kite. 109 bpm → 111 bpm @ *c.* 50″; 2′35″.

As befits Lennon's more wayward public persona, this song is irregular in a number of respects. Each stanza consists of seven lines of printed lyric, dividing 2 + 2 + 3. These divisions take unequal numbers of four-beat bars. Following three introductory bars, in verse 1, the pattern is 4 (for the first two lines) + 3 (for the next two) + 5 (for the last three lines), followed by two bars of instrumental filling. For verse 2, the pattern is 4 + 3 + 4. The interspersed waltz danced by Henry the horse takes 7 + 5 bars and is followed by one bar at the original tempo. The final verse again divides 4 + 3 + 4, while the extended playout divides 2 + 7 + 9. Against these three verses, however, the harmonic structure divides the song in two: verses 1 and 2 head from c to d, the waltz continues this to e, while verse 3 and the playout head again from c, through d, to e. This is summarized in Example 4.7. Note that both the verse and the waltz share

Ex. 4.7

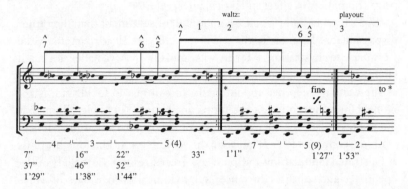

a structural 8-$\hat{7}$-6 in their respective keys (or $\hat{7}$-6-$\hat{5}$ if viewed from the perspective of the resultant, rather than initial, key). The turn to waltz-time in the interlude is rather literal, but George Martin's invention with calliope timbres keeps it vital, especially in light of the generally empty texture (harmonium line, kit, bass and voice during the verse). Note also the exactitude of McCartney's accompanying final line, a typical example of the care with which arrangements are executed. Lennon's dislike of the timbres of his own voice is legendary: his nasality here is well reflected in the calliope, while the eccentric mix which places him to the right (balancing the harmonium with bass and kit central) distances us from the (in)action and, in a sense, prepares the way for the chaotic playout cutups. These were created by taking recordings of calliope music already used, cutting them, throwing them on the floor and then splicing them randomly.[15] They can be more clearly heard on *Anthology 2*.

The song's position at the end of side one of the original album is considered important by most commentators. For Mellers, its atmosphere recalls the opening after songs exploring loneliness and togetherness, an atmosphere Riley finds Dickensian and rather sinister, providing a different view of freaks and misfits to that of 'Lucy': 'here the old-fashioned is bizarre, and the surreal downright spooky'.[16] Far from a simple translation of the original poster into song, MacDonald finds it elaborated with real wit (marked, perhaps, by the change from circus to fairground), although for Middleton, coming where it does in the journey, it proposes a false solidarity.

Interlude

It is at this point that a listener would have exchanged side one of the original LP for side two, and so it seems a suitable point to discuss those two songs which should have appeared on the album, but which were omitted by force of circumstances. The single release of 'Strawberry Fields forever' begins at about 91 bpm, increases slightly over the first minute, and lasts for a total of 4′04″. As it stands, it is one of a trio of Lennon's mid-period Beatle songs crucial to Britain's incipient psychedelia (the others being 'Tomorrow never knows' and 'I am the walrus'). The song did not start that way in Lennon's conception. There has long circulated a 'white label' bootleg cut of takes 1–7 and 25 (the final single spliced together takes 7 and 26), while take 1 (which lasts only 2′32″) and take 7 also appear on *Anthology 2*, in addition to Lennon's home-produced demo. These show that the song's refrain (which begins the single) arrived on the scene rather late, while Lennon's original conception had been of a gentle, fragile song.

The version as released consists of a short introduction, four refrains interspersed with three verses, and a somewhat unstructured coda which lasts for a quarter of the song and which makes use of both wild and tape-reversed drumming. It is perhaps this coda which most strongly captures the strangeness portrayed in the lyrics. The verses consist of two regular four-bar groups, moving from V through VI–V–IV to I. The refrains are less regular: six bars of $4/4$, one of $2/4$, one of $4/4$, one of $3/4$ and one bar (two in the cases of refrains 2 and 3) of $4/4$. Figure 4.4 indicates the most plausible grouping.

A: $|$I . . .$|$I . . .$|$V . . .$|$V . . .$|$VI* . . .$|$VI . . .$|$II .$|$VI . . .$|$IV . V$|$I . . .$|$(I . . .$|$)

    ⌞   2   ⌟ ⌞   4   ⌟ ⌞ 2   ⌟ ⌞   2 (3) ⌟

Fig. 4.4 The asterisked VI is later replaced by V^0

All the song's harmonies are major, with the brief exception of II (b) and VI (f♯), and the first V of the refrain. This e harmony accompanies the lyric 'down', its round vowel reinforcing the 'dark' flattened third of the melody (Lennon's demo had used 'back' for 'down', a far weaker vowel); it also underlies the song's general flatward tendency, manifested in cadentially prominent IVs and a mixolydian melody. The gravity of this change is the reason for the grouping boundary here, leaving the previous two bars to function as an extension of the verse's second four-bar group.

The first refrain and verse find Lennon accompanied by kit, bass, mellotron and a busy guitar, while the remainder uses an arrangement for trumpets and cellos. The story behind this serendipitous conjunction is well known. While takes 1 to 7 built the song up from Lennon's original solo guitar accompaniment to one for full band, Lennon remained dissatisfied with its busyness, asking Martin a week or so later to score it for trumpets and cellos,[17] a version which became take 26. The first version was in B♭, the second in C, but the differences in speeds were such that, when Martin agreed to Lennon's request to splice the two together (at 1′, on the entry of the second refrain), the fit was more than acceptable. It seems that the portentous nature of that mixolydian V is then amplified by the astonishing textures resulting from the second version. The cellos sound harsh and not quite synchronized, the trumpets are brash (these are partly the result of lowering the pitch by slowing the tape speed), and the empty spaces surrounding them induce a sense of vertigo.

Despite the connotations of strangeness which have grown up around the song (and which the lyrics do nothing to counter), a structural analysis can disinter an unchallenging regularity which seems closer to Lennon's original concept (and which enable the lyrics to be interpreted in terms of 'wonder' rather than 'fear'). Example 4.8 suggests that a very simple 3̂–2̂–1̂ motif can be found operating at three distinct levels: the surface (e.g. at the very beginning and end of the refrain), the refrain itself, and the refrain-plus-subsequent-verse. Its path at a middleground level is rather tortuous, moving through ♭2, but nevertheless secure. That the structure and its textural articulation seem almost to be moving counter to one another acts as a wonderful metaphor for Lennon's own uncertain sense of direction at the time.

'Penny Lane', the song's 'other', runs at 112 bpm, and lasts for 2′57″. Despite its very regular surface, it is a song founded on dualisms (and as such, seems in every way the obverse of 'Strawberry Fields forever'). The verse consists of two eight-bar strains (let us call them *a* and *a′*), harmonically identical but for the eighth bar. This is succeeded by an eight-bar refrain (*b*). The song then consists of three verses/refrains,

Ex. 4.8

with a final repeat of the refrain. This regularity is not immediately apparent: the entry of the piccolo trumpet at the beginning of the second strain of verse 2 suggests a thirty-two-bar song format (*aa'ba*), with the solo beginning a second verse. It is only at the eighth bar of this solo, with the trumpet reaching for high E♭, that the ruse becomes apparent.

The first dualism concerns the lyrics: MacDonald notes that the scene described is both summer and winter, raining and shining. Other dualisms depend on melodic and harmonic details. The first half of the verse (I–VI–IV–(II–)V–I on I) and the refrain (I–I♭–IV on mixolydian VII) are based on standard harmonic sequences, while the second half of the verse is both more static and chromatic. (See Ex. 4.9. Note that, although both MacDonald and Riley give the key as B, I agree with Mellers in hearing it as a slightly sharp B♭.) The first half of the verse is also accompanied by repeated flute and oboe chords registrally above the piano: these winds are absent from the chromatic harmonies, which therefore appear smoother. Additionally, the chromatic harmonies are associated with those parts of the lyrics describing 'very strange' happenings: the banker's disdain for waterproof clothing, the fireman's fussiness and the nurse's self-doubt.

McCartney's melody is founded on two small motifs. The first is the $\hat{3}$–$\hat{4}$–$\hat{5}$ motion which directs the background (and which makes sense of the upward transposition on the final refrain, from mixolydian VII to I – see again Ex. 4.9). This initially appears locally, as the opening D combines with the octave distant E♭–F at the end of bar 2, prior to the entry of the chromatic harmonies. Note that the melodic tonic (B♭) is never supported by a tonic harmony (as with 'She's leaving home'), strengthening the role of D ($\hat{3}$). The second is the double-skip melody, prominent both

Ex. 4.9

at the very beginning of the verse (overlapped, i.e. D–B♭–G and B♭–G–E♭), twice in the refrain (from E♭ and from C) and then in the final refrain (from F).

Riley believes the version released as a single sounds unfinished. Indeed, the cut released to DJs for radio play contained an extra trumpet phrase at the end, coming to rest on D (this can be heard on the *Anthology 2* version). The decision to cut this phrase seems to me to be structurally preferable. Without it, the last melodic pitches heard are an upper F and inflected D from McCartney, and a piano B♭ (eventually underpinned by I), reinforcing the structural close of the final refrain. With it, this elegant closure is left slightly in doubt.

The track contains prominent roles for orchestral instruments – flutes, oboes and brass, including the telling solo piccolo trumpet, together with carefully overdubbed pianos – whose parts were apparently arranged by Martin from suggestions sung by McCartney.[18] Indeed, Lennon and Harrison could almost have been absent, while Starr's part is far from prominent. Although both sides of the single resulted from a shared plan, this record illustrated the growing chasm between Lennon and McCartney. The brightness of the melody is echoed by the treble timbres – upper woodwinds, piccolo trumpet, high bass guitar, treble-dominant voice – which combined to create a celebration of English suburbia that proved to be powerful in setting English popular music free from its blues roots (and was speedily picked up during 1967 by the Kinks' 'Waterloo sunset', the Move's 'I can hear the grass grow', Traffic's 'Hole in my shoe', Keith West's 'Excerpt from a teenage opera', etc.).

Within you without you. 62 bpm; 5′4″.

On a number of grounds, this song is crucial to the album as a whole. With the exception of the later 'Revolution 9' (which appears on the loosely constructed album *The Beatles*, also known as *The White Album*), its sound-world is further from the rest of the Beatles' output than anything else, and of the group only Harrison plays on and was involved in the recording. For a song which once sounded so strange, its structure is oddly conventional: two verses (beginning at 32″ and 1′16″) and refrain (2″), instrumental break (2′23″), third verse (3′48″) and final refrain (4′34″). Harrison's command of the quasi-Indian medium is of a very high order. To begin with, the song is not thought harmonically (as all pop songs were unfailingly), but melodically, as befits the genre. This is made clear by Harrison's melody: the scale is C mixolydian (i.e. C–D–E–F–G–A–B♭–C) and, although the melody of the verse rises from and descends to a low E (part of an implied C tonic triad, perhaps), the refrain melody ascends from the notes F–A and finally comes to rest upon D, while the highest pitches extend to E♭–F (1′48″), taking the previous B♭–C (1′05″) a fourth higher. The strength and contoural peak of the B♭ in the melody (e.g. *talk*ing' and '*peo*ple' in verse 1, and '*life* flows' in the refrain) bespeaks the quiet certainty of the lyrics (the upper 'tonic' C is not needed in support), while the topmost F pities those people who might act 'if they only knew'. To match this, the song has an undeveloped sense of metre. The tabla pattern suggests four beats to the bar (see Ex. 4.10), but this metrical sense is present only in the verse, and even there sometimes weakly. The first verse closes with 4½ beats, the second with 5, and the third with 9½, while the refrain appears as an unmetred succession of 25 and then 20+ beats. Although the break (MacDonald calls it a 'gat')[19] may sound 'authentic', it is based not upon the opening scale and rhythmic pattern (as a Hindustani *gat* would be), but is a direct repeat (with a few ornamentations) of the melody of the verse, transferred to 5/8 time.

Responses to this track have been extremely varied, although its 'remarkable' (Goldstein) or 'slick' (Riley) nature is accepted even by detractors. Goldstein found the lyrics dull and dismal, and Riley is unable to see how it fits within the album. Other writers may be called upon to answer him: for Peyser it summarizes the entire first side in

Ex. 4.10

focusing on 'the space between us all and the people who hide themselves behind a wall of illusion';[20] for Middleton it is the key song on the album, destroying the alienation of side one through its detachment and serenity in an attitude of acceptance. MacDonald, too, insists on its rightness, calling it the album's conscience, the necessary sermon within the community singing. It is perhaps easier to see its place with the benefit of many years' distance and the ensuing hegemony of the Thatcherite megeneration.

When I'm sixty-four. 140 bpm; 2'37″.

The general atmosphere of McCartney's little song for his beloved father is created well by Martin's delicious clarinet arrangement and intensified by Ringo's resort to brushes, while what Mellers terms its 1920s music hall style (à la George Formby) can be traced through two factors. Firstly, there is the quality of McCartney's voice, the intensification of whose treble qualities indicates that the original vocal track has been speeded up to raise the pitch, probably by a tone. Whereas in 'Being for the benefit of Mr Kite', Lennon had been sidelined to the left of the stereo image, it is McCartney who now occupies this space. Secondly, there is the harmonic pattern. The song's | I–V | V–I | | I–IV | chromaticism–I | |, although by no means the most common ragtime sequence, none the less underpins Scott Joplin's *Rag-Time Dance* of 1906 and can be traced to Strauss's *Blue Danube* waltz. It could probably be followed through into examples of the work of John Philip Sousa and Henry Hall – we might recall that McCartney's father led an amateur jazz band. The song's structure is a simple alternation of verse and bridge: the verse is 8 + 8 bars (e.g. beginning at 11″ and 25″), while the bridge is 8 + 9 (e.g. 38″ and 52″): the nine-bar segment is best thought of as a final extension of two bars, the first of these being elided with bar 8. The first bridge slides a few verbal musings into the clarinet melody, while the second bridge paints a more complete picture of contented, if impecunious, retirement. This is yet another example of McCartney's

Ex. 4.11

selective, but well-judged attention to commonplace detail. McCartney's voice is positive throughout (Goldstein's jibe that this is fantasy retirement rather than mockery of aged comfort is probably right), reaching boldly for high E (note the untroubled octave rise) and three times slipping back to the tonic, each fall more secure than the previous (see Ex. 4.11). These falls are again crucial to the structure of the refrain, first in the context of VI, then of I. Note also the motif C–B–A, reversed in the bridge, and also the growing importance of A–G, from the introductory doodlings through to its VI, I and IV, I contexts in the refrain.

MacDonald points out that one crucial factor in the Beatles' success was their versatility, which far outstretched that of any of their rivals. This is nowhere more evident than in these first two songs of side two, where a genuine Indian – pop synthesis gives way to an equally genuine ragtime – pop synthesis. However, in the way that it appears to be aimed at parents (or even grandparents), this song was not particularly well received by the Beatles' usual audience. The complementary nature of young and old which Middleton finds in the song, and which begins to confirm their solution to the problem posed by the album, was not valued at a time of growing youth hegemony in popular culture. Yet again, the Beatles seem to have been ahead of their time.[21]

Lovely Rita. 85 bpm; 2'41".

This song is regarded as something of a throwaway: Riley's talk of whimsical inconsequentiality and Mellers's reference to perfunctoriness provide an apt summary. Despite these views, the song has a very strong sense of harmonic direction, traversing cycles of fifths either side of the tonic E. It has two main structural units, a verse and a refrain, but both use a mixture of dominant- and subdominant-based harmonies. The structure has a regularity not perhaps perceived on the surface. It begins with an eight-bar introduction (the latter four bars, beginning at 11", introduce backing vocals) and a four-bar refrain (beginning at 22") which, using I, IV and V, suggest normative lengths. The subsequent verse consists of 3 bars (33") + 4 (41") on I, IV, VII and III, while the second refrain is three bars long (52") on I, VI, II and V. This makes us realize, in retrospect, that the first refrain's four bars were really 3 + 1. Four bars of vocalizing Lennon lead to George Martin's four-bar honky-tonk/barrelhouse piano solo, and the 3 + 4 pattern set-up continues throughout the song. The jaunty quality suggested by these three-bar units contributes to what Mellers discusses as Rita's lack of emotional commitment.

The distinction between verse and refrain is continued in the melodic lines. The refrain is typical McCartney: there is an emphasis on rising contours and a virtuoso use of range, although ascents and descents are in fact nicely balanced, moving first to the flat-side, then to the sharp-side. The resultant line reaches down to E (see Ex. 4.12) in a similar way to the previous song, sinking below the tonic in the verse but retrieving it as part of the tonic arpeggiation at the beginning of the subsequent refrain. The verse sounds more like Lennon in its obvious focus on a succession of single pitches, but it plays its part within this structure. It also moves flatwards first and then sharpwards, but more time is spent in the first area. Despite this characteristic, MacDonald suggests that the verse evinces an exuberant interest in life (more mainstream culture according to Middleton), perhaps in contrast to Lennon's normal pose. The strongly rising melodic surface seems to afford such an interpretation.

Ex. 4.12

The final 30″ of the song are built on an unrelated harmony (a) and feature a new texture focused on piano, but including Lennon's beloved vocal explorations, in what sounds like a rather extended jam (of the sort the Beatles would increasingly indulge in over the next year or so in the studio). It is probably best to interpret the ending in historical terms, although the song itself offers two possibilities: either a turn from its exuberance in disgust (as Lennon perhaps later did),[22] or as a continuation and development of Lennon's accompanying vocals into background effects (mouth popping, 'chooka chooka', etc.) situated precisely behind McCartney in the mix. These might be interpreted as whimsical, although they seem to me rather more like an undermining of the song's geniality.

These last 30″ seem to increase the distance travelled in the song from the opening, which emphasizes a treble-rich strummed guitar to the left of the mix (which is thereafter relegated somewhat), to what appears like a doubling of tempo on the entry of McCartney's voice (a doubling constantly counteracted by Lennon's recounting of the song's title), to even faster surface movement at the end, but over an unchanging chord.

Good morning good morning. 121 bpm; 2′41″.

If the three-bar units in 'Lovely Rita' felt strange, this song feels stranger still, being the only song on the album to do violence to the very idea of the normative four-beat bar. This is encapsulated in the difficulty Ringo Starr seems to have in finding a suitable pattern: with the exception of sections which do fall more regularly (e.g. from 45″), he tends to treat each beat equally. In my estimation, the barring works as follows in verse

1: the verse itself divides into four lines, starting at 12″, 16″, 22″, 27″ with the refrain starting at 30″; these lines in turn divide into beats, as shown in Figure 4.5, where the syllable on each downbeat is also given.

3 + 3 + 4	'Noth-'; 'save'; 'call'
3 + 5 + 4	'Noth-'; 'what'; 'been'
5 + 4	'Noth-'; 'you'
3 + 3	'noth-'; 'it's'
4 + 4	'morn-'

Fig. 4.5

It is only in the refrain (that rather ironic '*good* morning') that normality is recovered. The strangeness is used to reinforce the notion of this as an outsider's song: everybody else in the singer's world is comfortable. Indeed, it would not be difficult to iron out these inconsistencies and translate it into regular four-beat bars throughout (but with what a significant loss of effect!). In this context, the (relieved) break into a standard shuffle pattern at 45″ and 1′27″ seems to intensify Lennon's irony, as does the melodic line. The song is in Lennon's beloved blues-recalling mixolydian on A, with a limited range which sinks from A to E in all but the third of four strains (see Ex. 4.13). At the end, however, when we have 'good morning good morning good', the final word leaps back to the tonic A in a sort of mock (but exceedingly false) resolution. The extensions ('everybody knows' and 'people running') concentrate on the upper C♯-D pair which had appeared as the upbeat to the fourth of the verse's lines.

As with so many of the songs on the album, 'Good morning good morning' has a surprisingly sparse texture: there is only a very weakly strummed guitar, kit and bass to accompany Lennon to the left, with occasional guttural saxes to the right and the centrally spaced brittle guitar solo. The physical presence created by Lennon's voice is, however, immense.

The standard interpretation of this song is of Lennon's anger at the mindless existences of everyday humanity, hence Riley's vision of an aggressive and ironic workaday nightmare, supported particularly by the snare fills (ab 54″ and 1′36″). This may also account for the return of ambient sound-effects (from the farmyard, of course) and the very raw sax arrangement. MacDonald takes only a slightly different line, declaring that nobody could be offended by Lennon's splenetic gusto, which is

Ex. 4.13

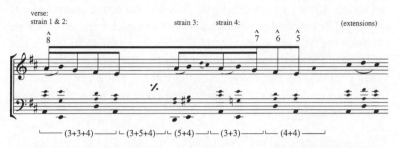

emphasized by Martin's compression of the signal of the entire song (a technique found to different effect and for different reasons on earlier Motown recordings), that emphasizes treble frequencies. For MacDonald, the song belies the album's subsequent, rather airy-fairy reputation.

Neither Mellers nor Middleton take this line. For Mellers, there is no anger or even any irony in the good morning – it is simply morning, and as such is necessarily good. Mere being is sufficient. Middleton follows this line in suggesting that the song displays rebirth (after the confusions of side one and the cleansing of 'Within you without you') with a new innocence, accepting all, even the despised 'Meet the Wife'. In all probability, this is the only successful way to interpret the song within its context.

Sgt. Pepper's Lonely Hearts Club Band (reprise). 116 bpm; 1′18″.

And so, after a half hour's excursion through a large variety of different scenes and ideas, we return to our seats among the imaginary audience although, as Middleton insists, we have learnt from our experiences: for him this song is a re-creation of the opening, but without regression. This is clearly marked by the new tempo (an increase of more than 20 per cent), the strength of the beat and, as MacDonald points out, the almost tangible excitement in the studio, beginning right from McCartney's count-in (but what should we make of Lennon's initial ironic 'byee'?). Structurally, we are left with the heart of the earlier song, though it is heard a tone lower. The omission of the song's earlier rock sections (with the exception of the fusion attempted in the central section) would be remarkable in its coincidence if it were not that something like Middleton's suggestion was present in the Beatles' collective compositional strategy. The insistence on Sgt. Pepper's loneliness begins to suggest an exit from the false persona of the album: Sgt. Pepper may be lonely, but the verve of the performance makes it clear that his band is not. For such a strong rocker, it is surprising that Riley interprets the upward shift (to the original key) at 43–45″ as respect for the Tin Pan Alley traditions in which such a shift was a cliché.

A day in the life. 77 bpm → 82/164 bpm @ 2′21″; 5′2″ (5′33″).

The last chord has not died, however, before the entry of a solitary acoustic guitar on offbeat quavers, and the innocent listener is led into one of the most harrowing songs ever written. Its structure is well known: Lennon's original material moves through three verses (10, 9 and 9½ bars), to the first orchestral crescendo, McCartney's serendipitous insertion, Lennon's floating vocalize, a fourth verse and the final crescendo and landing. All the reports mention that, originally, no one was sure how to connect Lennon's opening to McCartney's middle, and so twenty-four bars were left to be filled in later. These begin on the words 'love to' (1′39″). They can actually be counted (and heard on the *Anthology 2* version, together with McCartney's experimental piano clusters), although Starr's beat becomes submerged at various points, particularly towards the end. In order to do so, however, it is necessary that they be counted at twice the speed of the beat I have given. Normally, a rock four-beat bar can be found with the snare sounding on the second and fourth beats (giving a speed of 77 bpm in this instance). The Beatles were clearly counting with the snare on the third beat (i.e. at 154 bpm) which is an interesting aside suggesting that this norm still remained fluid in 1967. The presence of the beat during these bars shows how total was its domination even in such an experimental setting. The link between popular music and dance has not been severed at this historical point.

There are no immediately obvious links between the verses and the interpolation (although numerous commentators have supplied them).[23] Musically, they work partly on hypermetric grounds: Lennon's verses are built from five two-bar units (at 77 bpm), although the last unit is foreshortened in all but the first verse. McCartney's insertion is formed from a succession of four five-bar units (at double speed, i.e. 164 bpm, although the fourth unit loses its last bar), and the subsequent 'dream sequence' (beginning at 2′49″) consists of a further two five-bar units at the original speed. Thus, '5' figures as normative (rather than the ubiquitous '4'), both giving coherence to the song and enabling what I shall argue is the most fundamental aspect of its 'meaning', of which more later.

Harmonically, the verses all wander from G towards e, frequently via C, as if in a never-ending but ultimately unsuccessful attempt to accentuate the positive. The interpolation transmutes e into a positive E with mixolydian touches, until the dream sequence restores the original area with total effortlessness. Melodically, Lennon's verses hang between B and upper E, while McCartney's middle occupies the inverse, from B to lower E, setting up a sound-world that is immediately blown away by Lennon's re-entry on upper E and shifting higher. Unusually it is Lennon's verse which, beneath the static melodic surface, suggests middleground arpeggiations of e (rather than the tonic G!), while McCartney's interpolation, beneath a mobile surface, remains focused on a small scalar motion. Example 4.14 suggests that the stasis of the melodic B is fundamental (balanced as it is between upper and lower Es), not least in its successive reharmonizations (by G, e, C, A, eventually F, and ultimately even B!). The interpolation retains the B/lower E (from the verse), while the structural line falls pentatonically through A and F♯ to E at the beginning of the vocalize. In the final verse, the structural line retrieves B by way of what, in verse 1, had been notes of secondary importance.[24]

The richness (and extreme rightward placing) of Lennon's voice in the opening verse (with added echo) highlights the thinness of the accompaniment: bass and leftward simple strummed guitar, minimal piano and maracas. The entry of the kit after the first line of verse 2 (a subtlety later to become a trademark of the band Jethro Tull) promises much, and ultimately leads to the orchestral chaos. The orchestra is introduced so subtly, low down on the right beneath a fading Lennon, that we are hardly aware that it has not been present all along. McCartney's interpolation continues the texture, but the increase of speed sug-

Ex. 4.14

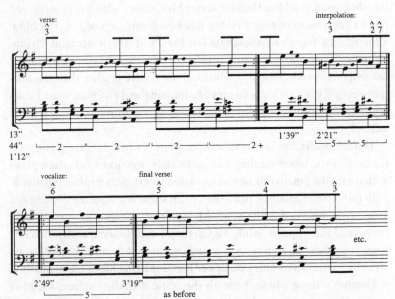

gests a thickening, which is fulfilled by the brass entry during the dream sequence. The final verse has left and right channels switched, as if the interpolation has really counted, has really changed something (and, if my interpretation of the melody carries any weight, it has). The very last minute is an astonishing experience. The final chord is sounded at 4′21″. At 4′50″ it is possible to hear the creaking of a piano stool (the first real intimation on the album that we are hearing real, lived time), at 5′02″ the faders are pulled down and then, at 5′11″ we enter 22″ of Lennon's beloved meaninglessness (on the original album, this was the playout groove, and so would continue for ever until the turntable arm was removed).

That much was comparatively easy to write dispassionately. But the immensity of the horror that this song's lyrics seem to portray demands attention, and two paths are fruitful. Even writers unmoved by the remainder of the album will speak eloquently of what this song means to them. Richard Goldstein, for instance, whose early criticism I have already mentioned, wrote of its 'seminal influence' and its profundity, readily received by its entire audience. A great deal is made of the line

'I'd love to turn you on', and its superficially apparent call to drug use. While acknowledging Lennon's use of LSD while writing, the song itself is far from the call to intoxication it was taken to be: it is already a warning against this option, although much less obvious than that of 'Within you without you'. Middleton argues that the song investigates hallucination, but rejects drug use. In the stylistic context of rock, those massive, indeed horrifying (this was 1967, after all), orchestral crescendi must be interpreted as discouragement, perhaps illustrating the result of such use. Countering those interpretations which see the song as summarizing the entire album (the carefully planned killer album idea I earlier discounted), MacDonald points out that "A day in the life" was only the second song to be recorded, before many of the others had even been thought about. Indeed, even its placement on the album was fortuitous: according to Martin, there was no other song which could follow that long fadeout.[25]

A meaning can be disinterred for the song itself. MacDonald is full of ideas: 'A song not of disillusionment with life itself but of disenchantment with the limits of mundane perception, "A day in the life" depicts the "real" world as an unenlightened construct that reduces, depresses, and ultimately destroys', and yet it still offers a transcendent optimism in our own power to develop a beautiful construct. Riley is equally eloquent, even questioning whether Lennon's verses are dreaming McCartney's everyman, or vice versa. Middleton, too, finds the song an apt conclusion to the album, noting that its complexity and equivocation offer an impressively intelligent exploration of our cultural problem: 'we can no more run away from our civilization than we can be content with it as it stands'. This near-denial of ultimate hope was brilliantly captured in Goldstein's early review where, focusing on verses 2 and 3, he observes the narrator subdued by total despair, while the crowd (every-*man* again?) looks, but simply turns away untouched (with particular reference to Eliot's *The Waste Land*). The song's subject is, thus, an intensely counter-cultural one, one couched specifically in terms of a flight from banality, but as ever the Beatles are equivocal about the outcome. Mellers insists, in this vein, on the sublime understatement of 'rather sad' in verse 1.[26]

We can, then, say what this song is probably about. We can declare that, however partially, it is reducible to mere words. To do so, however, seems to me a cardinal mistake. Mellers offers an alternative approach when he claims that the song is not about what it refers to. Indeed, these references confuse rather than clarify, and we might argue that, in attempting to clarify them, critics are ultimately misrepresenting the song and, hence, the entire album. For Mellers, the song is about the contrast between its simple tune and the horrific events depicted by the words. That contrast can be felt to operate on a number of levels: terrifying/grotesque, illusion/reality, inner/outer. This seems to me to be a fruitful approach, for we might say that if the Beatles had been able to 'clarify' what the song was about (and a similar comment can be applied to many of the other songs on the album), then they would have done so. What is important is that the meaning could only be presented in the unclarified manner that it was, a manner that is ultimately beyond straightforward presentation.

There is another (perhaps less hackneyed) way to make the same point. In the context of the setting (unequivocally false but presented none the less: 'we're listening to a pretend audience that is pretending to listen to the pretend Sgt. Pepper's Lonely Hearts Club Band')[27] – a setting which presents itself to us as unreal but which is closed as an experiential whole by the astounding reprise of the title track – 'A day in the life', being external, can only be unreal to that unreality, i.e. utter and devastating reality (a reality founded musically on units of '5' rather than '4'). No matter how strange and disturbing the elements of the song seem to be (the curious references, the odd grouping, the crescendi, the piano fade and playout groove, the dislocation of the interpolation), *that is our reality* is what the song is really about. Resistance to exegesis is the only valid option.

This becomes, of course, a much larger question which I shall do no more than lay out here. We know that McCartney and Lennon (at least) had some sort of 'meaning' in mind when constructing the album. McCartney's meaning hinges on the device of the package, Lennon's on exploring (but simultaneously hiding) his personal (and certainly not everyone else's) response to occurrences. In asking how legitimate it is to make the album take on a meaning over and above these (which most critics have undertaken, perhaps most particularly Middleton and Whiteley), we are questioning the extent to which it can be used to succour our own world views. In other words, rather than the interpretation being the clear glass through which *Sgt. Pepper* can be properly seen, the obverse is much more nearly true.[28] And, of course, in listening, we are all necessarily interpreters.

The sheer versatility and stylistic diversity of the material on the album was, and remains, astonishing. McCartney set out to defeat the Beach Boys at what was becoming their own game and, without question, succeeded. The 'package' concept, clichéd now, was brilliantly original. Not only did we have the gatefold sleeve and printed lyrics (inviting us into what was portrayed as a closed coterie), but the badges, the false moustache and Sgt. Pepper stripes that were supplied as cutouts suggested we could all the more easily pretend to be in the band. This much remains, even if McCartney's original packaging was simply economically unviable. The concept was also historically vital (see chapter 6) and Peter Blake's execution so provocative as to have encouraged its own pastiches (most notably that of iconoclast Frank Zappa's 1968 'reply', *We're Only in it for the Money*). Even this opens up differing interpretations: Riley views the sleeve in terms of the Beatles attending the funeral of their former image, a concept he sees as rather superficial, while Tom Phillips[29] saw all the album's 'performers' were on the cover, exactly as one would have expected from a 1967 album cover. With the benefit of historical hindsight, we might actually find a disjunction between the cover and the album it contains. Mr Kite is there in his gaudiness, perhaps, Sgt. Pepper to be sure, and presumably Billy Shears and Lucy, but Lovely Rita would perhaps have felt out of her depth ('chuck'), and as for the composers as schoolboys, DIY enthusiasts or gurus . . . No, for all its merits, the face the album presents to the world, still, is not a representation of what it hides.

The originality of the album extended further, of course. Dave Harker notes that, in comparison to the £400 expended on their first album, *Sgt. Pepper* cost £25,000 to make; and yet the Beatles still saw only a little under 8½ per cent of the takings, compared to more than 47 per cent to EMI, nearly 30 per cent to retailers and nearly 16 per cent in tax to the government.[30] Those MBEs were certainly paid for.

5

Reception

The immediate reception accorded *Sgt. Pepper* took three forms. The general public had a little advance warning of the album: the erstwhile jazz paper *Melody Maker* announced the title on 22 April 1967, while on 6 May both main British music papers (*Melody Maker* and the more pop-orientated *New Musical Express*) gave advance notice of the running order. The latter also proclaimed that the disc would not be banded, so that it would play in a 'virtually continuous' fashion. So begins the myth of the unity of *Sgt. Pepper*. By this time, the Beatles had already completed most of the work on *Magical Mystery Tour*.

A week prior to public release, journalists were gathered at Brian Epstein's home for a 'listen-in', avidly reported in both *Melody Maker* and *New Musical Express* on 27 May. Thereafter, published interest is strangely patchy. In the *NME*'s undated 'Summer Special', journalist Andy Gray complained that by spending as long as three months working on an album, the Beatles 'soon become forgotten'. *NME*'s Allen Evans reviewed the album on 20 May (clearly on only one hearing, judging from the superficial quality of the response), the *Times*'s William Mann on 29 May, *Melody Maker*'s Chris Welch on 3 June and the *Sunday Times*'s Derek Jewell on 4 June, followed by general publications such as the *New Statesman* (Wilfrid Mellers, 2 June)[1] and, in the USA, the *New York Times* (Richard Goldstein, 18 June), *Village Voice* (Tom Phillips, 22 June) and *Newsweek* (Jack Kroll, 26 June) by the end of the month. Most of these reviews are positive, ranging from Evans's bland; 'No one can deny that the Beatles have provided us with more musical entertainment, which will both please the ear and get the brain working a bit, too!' to Mellers's considered view that the album is so moving because 'bits of tune . . . seem the younger, more vulnerable in a world to which the simple solidarities of good old Sgt. Pepper no longer apply'. The notable

58

exception (other than some correspondence to *Melody Maker* which may well have come from jazz enthusiasts) was Goldstein, for whom the album was consolidatory rather than exploratory, obsessed with production and shoddy in composition. His indictment was damning: it was an 'album of special effects, dazzling but ultimately fraudulent'. This review immediately incurred the wrath of Phillips, for whom the album's novel-like metaphorical structure made it their most ambitious and successful yet. Later, in 1981, Robert Christgau claimed that Goldstein's panning had at the time no constituency, although many critics would now agree with him.[2]

This coverage is small, especially within the music press, compared to the column inches expended at the time on the Beach Boys, the Monkees, current British pop sensation Procol Harum, and others, although it may well have been larger than that of any other single album. In 1967, the album was not the major marketing device it is today: bands still relied on singles. It would not be until the following two years, and the growing strength particularly of Cream and Led Zeppelin, that the album format began to claim centre stage. Beyond simple reviews, coverage was limited to such things as the page 1 advertisement on the 3 June issue of *NME*, and the report in the same paper of 22 April of the (comparatively) massive costs of the album. Among a wider audience, however, interest was huge, and growing disillusion with the Beatles within the print media was probably not matched by the public at large. Every author cites a different instance, from 'rich older women' who sang snatches at dinner parties and reports of the effect on US bands, to American journalist Langdon Winner's famous report of a long drive on 2 June 1967, the day of the album's US release, where it was almost the only thing played on any radio station. Its release was described as a major cultural event, distilling the spirit of 1967, while in Mann's review it acted to summarize pop music to date, being 'chiefly significant as constructive criticism . . . examining trends and tidying up inconsistencies and undisciplined work'. Stokes insisted that it was a cultural milestone; Poirier claimed that 'listening to the *Sgt. Pepper* album one thinks not simply of the history of popular music but of the history of this century'; while the critic Kenneth Tynan went even further, suggesting that its release was 'a decisive moment in the history of western civilization'. In the light of such widely felt euphoria, it was hardly surprising for Greil

Marcus later to claim that, by 1968, the album seemed hollow, 'a triumph of effects', as American life turned sour, both politically and socially. Stokes notes that the US establishment had been far more distrustful of the album than the British, right from the start.[3] With the benefit of three decades' hindsight, opinion seems to be that, although not their best album musically, it was culturally crucial, a distinction I find increasingly strange, and to which I shall return.

So, what is *Sgt. Pepper* about? Interpretations fall into four broad categories. The most frequently cited, if also the most problematic, is the view of *Sgt. Pepper* as clarion call for the nascent counter-culture's exhortation to 'tune in, turn on, drop out'. As early as 27 May, both music press and national dailies were reporting the BBC's ban on 'A day in the life' on the grounds that the line 'I'd love to turn you on' was an incitement to drug taking. (McCartney's immediate denial was carried by *Melody Maker* on 27 May.) As George Melly was later to argue, what was notable was that they 'presented drug culture in so desperate a light'[4] – far more insightful to recognize 'A day in the life' as an urgent call to turn on to 'life'. For MacDonald, the psychedelic experience was simulated, but not as a form of wishful thinking.

What should be recognized is that *Sgt. Pepper* was produced within a drug culture, to the extent that Lennon was regularly using LSD and marijuana by 1966, with the other Beatles to a lesser extent. US writers, in particular, are in no doubt about the drug-related content of songs on the album. Thus Pichaske explains, with no trace of irony, the references to 'I get high' on 'With a little help from my friends', 'take some tea' (a synonym for 'pot') on 'Lovely Rita' and 'digging the weeds' on 'When I'm sixty-four'. Poirier offers a different list, finding such references in 'With a little help from my friends', 'Lucy in the sky with diamonds', 'Fixing a hole' and 'A day in the life'.[5] More importantly, Poirier insists that the meanings of these songs do not *reduce* to such references. The warning does not appear to have been heeded by possibly the most sustained and considered drug-infused interpretation, that by Sheila Whiteley. Rather than simply suggest that references to drugs can be found in some of the lyrics, she argues that the experience of using LSD is literally *encoded* in the music, indeed in all songs on the album with the exception of 'She's leaving home', 'Lovely Rita' and 'When I'm sixty-four'. (Presumably she too finds Pichaske's interpretations somewhat superficial.) Although she declares that their 'precise meaning . . . remains conjectural', a point which I shall take up below, she believes that the conjunction of particular verbally invoked images with various timbral manipulations in the studio clearly evoke the LSD experience. Nowhere is this clearer than in 'Lucy'. She tells us: 'everyday experience: "Picture yourself . . ." is transformed into an evocative sign through the intensification of the unusual visual experience: "With tangerine trees . . .". The singer takes on the role of the experienced user and in the verse leads the novice . . . into a changed reality.' And, although even this interpretation should not necessarily be read as a recommendation to encounter LSD, Shapiro reminds us that the album clearly did increase the interest in LSD and in psychedelia generally (even among non-users).[6]

Whether such an interest in drugs signified a deeper commitment to counter-cultural values is a more problematic point: Whiteley is concerned less that the album set the agenda for counter-cultural response than that it offered optimistic escapism.[7] At Epstein's promotional dinner party, Norrie Drummond spotted Harrison wearing the badge of the New York Workshop of Non Violence – a yellow submarine out of which grew flowers; but LSD-guru Timothy Leary's identification of the Beatles as avatars for the new world order was already well known. McCartney seems surprised at this appropriation: 'I don't think changing the world was really in our minds. I think it came as a surprise to find that people thought that we were changing the world.' Whiteley insists that eight of the songs 'confront the problems of the outside world and propose and celebrate the counter-cultural alternative'. Dave Harker, on the other hand, lambasts the album and the technological developments it ushered in for their encouragement of the privatized experience, now symbolized by listening through headphones, in direct opposition to the communal values espoused by the counter-culture. Here, of course, we need to realize that such interpretations are not innocent, that (what I read as) Whiteley's fan-turned-musicologist and Harker's SWP identities are inevitably implicated. In its explicit, prescient call to the me-generation, perhaps 'Within you without you' is a key track (although Whiteley is again keen to find 'a link with cannabis'), expressing the deepest commitment to the counter-culture.[8]

Developments of this hermeneutic strategy concentrate on the importance within *Sgt. Pepper* of illusion as an exploration of 'the human condition' (and if that doesn't make it Art, then nothing will). Joan Peyser puts it concisely, arguing that the album's potency lies in its discovery that humanity cannot live without illusion but that, as the last song shows, neither can we live with it. Tim Riley's explanation is similar: the album argues the necessities of fantasies, and simultaneously the danger of indulging in them. Jack Kroll's early review foregrounded this issue. He declared it 'useless to lament the simple old days of the Mersey sound . . . loss of innocence is increasingly their theme and the theme of more "serious" new art'. He cites Harold Pinter in this latter context.[9]

Indeed, it appears in retrospect that with *Sgt. Pepper* the cultural legitimization of popular music is already complete, an issue to which I shall return in the final chapter. In declaring that the Beatles' desire to 'turn you on' is 'a desire to start the bogged-down juices of life itself', Kroll declares the song their 'Waste Land'. Loneliness as a theme is picked up by Pichaske, and also by Goldstein's later interpretation of 'A day in the life',[10] as noted in chapter 4. Mellers puts a different gloss on this; considering the 'leery laugh' at the close of 'Within you without you', he notes Harrison's dismissive explanation – 'after all that long Indian stuff you want some light relief . . . It's true, but it's still a joke . . . It's serious and it's not serious' – and argues that the music was easily appropriated by its generation because its wariness of traditional values ('the young . . . won't . . . once more be taken in') does not mask its integrity ('their search for salvation . . . springs from the heart'). Mellers reads Harrison's ironic stance into the material: Lucy's up-tempo refrain; the rhyming incantation in 'With a little help from my friends'; the cello line and uncomprehending duologue of 'She's leaving home'.[11] In this early review he misses the irony of 'Good morning good morning', an irony other writers find crucial: Welch finds a 'self-mocking undercurrent', Kroll a deflation of the Beatles' own seriousness (which is how he reads that 'leery laugh'), while Poirier notes an appealing quality of self-parody. The necessary sophistication engendered by what Mellers takes to be the Beatles' aim also provides the ground on which most of its detractors attacked the album. Riley notes the self-conscious sophistication which led to its mistrust by purists (and also, subsequently, to Lennon's own unease, the album being far from his later autobiographical aesthetic). Gabree, who had previously criticized the Beatles' lack of political backbone, argues along Riley's lines, insisting (rather inconsistently, perhaps) that 'art must simply be true to itself'. Middleton, in probably the most thoroughgoing analysis of the metaphysical journey undertaken by the album's succession of tracks, argues that its outcome is far more positive, being about tradition and rebirth through the conflict between, and possible resolution of, the relationship between cultures. (Whiteley, perhaps necessarily, finds it wholly subversive of cultural norms.) The grounds for Middleton's analysis have been summarized in chapter 4, and so I will not continue with them here. Indeed, the album's success in treating this theme is probably also the reason for the mistrust Riley evinces.[12]

Some commentators have taken Middleton's point further, and argued that it is specifically English (or British) traditions which are encountered. Hatch and Millward point to the consistent use of indigenous content, references and imagery. Indeed, a list is not hard to assemble: 'Meet the Wife', parking meters, Billy Shears' club singer persona, the circus, preoccupation with school and the weather, railway porters, the Isle of Wight, Blackburn, the Albert Hall, etc. This is reflected in Jewell's suggestion that the Lennon–McCartney songs 'have the trait which music hall artists from Marie Lloyd to George Formby possessed of telling a story wryly or humorously, often with the cock bounce of the melody belying the sadness of the lyric', and in Chris Welch's similar observation that 'the Beatles have always loved telling a tale, sometimes sadly, sometimes with wry humour, often mixing de[p]ressing sentiments with a chirpy bounce in the grand music hall tradition . . . all the music retains the Beatle stamp of humour, sorrow, sympathy and cynicism'.[13] Of course, the Beatles give us what we might call metonymic transformations of social narratives rather than mere tales.[14] From a US perspective, similar points are made; for instance by Poirier, who finds the album a review of contemporary English life. This is supported by what appears to be an endearing provinciality: 'they respond with a participatory tenderness and joy to styles and artifacts [bringing an] absolutely unique kind of involvement . . . and of enjoying the knowledge'. Kroll concurs, in his reference to 'little lyrics, dramas and satires on homely virtues, homely disasters, homely people, and all the ambiguities of home'. In most cases, of course, it is more specifically northern imagery which is at issue, imagery which promotes northern provinciality over the best London can offer,[15] a tradition which might be traced from Formby and Gracie Fields through to the Smiths (e.g. 'Frankly Mr Shankly') and various bands of the 1980s (such as Happy Mondays).

Perhaps the most intractable interpretation concerns the unity of the *Sgt. Pepper* project. I shall return to this issue in chapter 6, but simply would like to note here how pervasive it is. On 6 May 1967, *NME* announced that the album would be 'virtually continuous' (in its near lack of spacing between tracks). This was followed by Kroll's review, in which he argues for its 'organicism'. William Mann's review in *The Times* suggests one basis for such an interpretation. He finds the album's shape and integrity founded on the reprise of the title track, and on the return to the same atmosphere found in 'Being for the benefit of Mr Kite', but on no more substantial base. Indeed, although the 'unity' of an album was a rare concept, he describes it as slightly specious. A second possible basis can be unearthed from Allen Evans's early review, where he hears all audience interjections as though they come from the same source (i.e. the live audience). As Tom Phillips declares; 'the band is the world of performance, a world within a world created by and for its audience'.[16] Thus, in all likelihood, Lennon's unease. Although roadie Neil Aspinall denied that it was ever intended as a 'concept', Ringo Starr was claiming in 1971 that it still made 'a whole concept'.[17] Roger McGuinn, lead member of the hippy cult band the Byrds, reports listening to the album in the 1980s and being surprised to find it had a lack of continuity he did not remember; while Martin was concerned immediately after its completion that this lack of continuity might make it sound pretentious. The generally negative account of Gabree declares such unity a 'sham' and Stokes, in describing the album as both a cultural milestone, and a breakthrough as an artefact (this is the factor which McCartney himself hoped would ensure its reception as a single 'package'), refers to the many 'ingenious exegeses from those who wanted it to be unified'.[18] Perhaps, and partly because its cultural impact was so large, it was simply being asked to do too much.

We have here, then, a range of interpretations as to the 'meaning' of *Sgt. Pepper*. None, I think, is particularly implausible. The problem surely lies (to paraphrase Poirier) in attempts to *reduce* the meaning of the album to one or other of these interpretations. Middleton came later to regard *Sgt. Pepper* as 'undercoded', in that it was received with 'general understanding' but without being tied to a specific 'meaning', i.e. in an analogous fashion to the way that much art music is received.[19] We might characterize such generality in suitably unspecific language by suggesting that *Sgt. Pepper* affords a looseness of perceptual clarity particularly through its lyrics, its images and the studio manipulation of its musical materials. Surely one of the reasons it has been valued is its very richness, and in attempting to choose between rival interpretations we begin to deny that which we most value.

Due to their individuality and sheer number, ordinary listeners have responses to which we cannot, in detail, be party. Critics and reviewers are paid to respond. Musicians, however, can comment on a developing tradition in highly creative ways. During the 1960s (and before the rise of 'rock' as such), the practice of making 'covers' was very common. Songs which were deemed likely to become popular would be recorded by 'mainstream' artists in blatant attempts to cash in on a song's anticipated popularity (and occasionally these even outsold the 'original'). Alan Walsh, writing in *Melody Maker* on 17 June 1967, noted with surprise that only three of the songs on *Sgt. Pepper* had been covered: 'With a little help from my friends' (Evans's review described it as a 'very pleasant beat-and-melody tune', identifying the characteristic which made it suitable for covering), 'When I'm sixty-four', and a single version of 'She's leaving home'. Walsh proposes that the reason for this lack of covers was that the sound of the album was more important than the identity of the individual songs. This was immediately recognized as a new factor. None the less, over the years, a variety of bands have found it worthwhile to add their musical commentary on *Sgt. Pepper*, and I consider a few of the most substantial here.

The release in November 1968 of Joe Cocker's cover of 'With a little help from my friends', and his performance at Woodstock, was the public's first widespread encounter with the singer's tortured, nicotine-soaked howl. This version played a part in the rise of 'blue-eyed' (i.e. white-skinned) soul which included songs by artists such as Delaney and Bonnie Bramlett, Leon Russell, Chicago, Blood, Sweat and Tears and, in the UK, Stevie Winwood and, slightly later, Eric Clapton. In its funereal shuffle pace (at a speed of about 46 bpm) and the portentous bass/guitar line of the bridge, Cocker's version seems to evoke the time dilation experienced under LSD. Such textures were to become one of the constituents of heavy rock in the late 1960s and early 1970s, especially through bands such as Vanilla Fudge and King Crimson. The balance between the sharp-side questions and the flat-side answers of the Beatles' original has been lost. The flat side has priority over the verse in a number of ways. We may characterize this flat side as 'rock', as opposed to 'pop', on account of the mixolydian VII.[20] Firstly, the flat-side sequence appears isolated in the introduction. Secondly, the backing during the verses is minimal (bass, almost inaudible held organ and underplayed kit), whereas during the refrains there is the full weight of organ, kit, heavy electric guitar and female voices. The security provided by this accompaniment means that Cocker can leave the lyrics of the refrain to the chorus, while he extemporizes over them in hallowed 'sanctified' gospel style. Here, then, the song has been totally transformed in terms of style and, perhaps, the 'friends' no longer seem as innocent as they were for the Beatles.

In November 1974 John Lennon came out of semi-retirement to perform a short set at an Elton John gig in New York singing, among other songs, 'Lucy in the sky with diamonds'; shortly after, Elton John's version was released as a single, with Lennon as backing vocalist. It begins with a remarkable coincidence: the speed (114 bpm as against 138 bpm) is slowed by 21 per cent, while the transposition from the key of A to G represents a drop in frequency of just 22 per cent; it is as though the slower speed is felt as a consequence of the lower pitch. As befits the production, it is larger in every respect. The instrumentation highlights tubular bells and various keyboards, enriching the glitter of Lucy's diamonds. The opening sequence is repeated four times (rather than the original single appearance) and is played on the larger-sounding guitar instead of the original harpsichord, thereby preparing us for the song's greater space and giving it greater gravity. The cymbal wash, the rich offbeat synthesizer chords, and the near lack of any bass in the verse convey a strong sense of Lucy 'floating'. Then, after the second refrain (maintaining the same proportional relationship to the verse), there is an organ solo which replays the first half of the verse, but at the tempo of the refrain and with the refrain's full band. This leads into a sung repeat of 'newspaper taxis', and then into a beautifully executed (and gleefully inauthentic) reggae version of the refrain. Thereafter, the remainder of the song is like the original, except for an extended playout which emphasizes the backing third above the tonic-prominent melody.

In the spring of 1988 *NME* put together a compilation, *Sgt. Pepper Knew My Father*, in which each track was taken by a different band of the late eighties. At the same time a single was released, which reached No. 1 in the British charts;[21] this coupled Wet Wet Wet's rather anaemic version of 'With a little help from my friends' and Billy Bragg's beautifully underplayed 'She's leaving home'. Bragg is well known as a post-punk singer-songwriter who has written songs with a similar tone (such as the stunning 'Levi Stubbs' Tears'). On 'She's leaving home', the Beatles' strings are replaced by a more solid Carole King-style piano, while in the refrain the title is taken by an ethereal synthesized string line, perhaps suggesting that the protagonist hasn't merely left home. Bragg's characteristic flat, unpolished Essex delivery is a revelation. His compassion is palpable but unsentimental, particularly on the internal rhymes (in verse 1, 'door/more', 'key/free') where Paul McCartney's unresolved $\hat{6}$ (over V) is always allowed to come to rest on $\hat{5}$. These two songs are the only ones on the album to be sung without heavy doses of irony, indicative of the lack of esteem in which the Beatles were held at the time.

Probably the most audacious covers were issued in 1992 when US fifties-style band Big Daddy issued their own *Sgt. Pepper's Lonely Hearts Club Band*: all thirteen songs are reworked in various Afro-American/mainstream pop-based 1950s styles. Here, then, we have a set of songs written in the mid-1960s, remade to sound as though they had originated in the 1950s, but unearthed more than three decades later. The remarkable aesthetic success of some of these must be seen as counter to the view that the songs of *Sgt. Pepper* were special because they were constituted by their sound, rather than the combination of their lyrics, melodies and harmonies. Overt references to actual 1950s hits abound, such as Jerry Lee Lewis's 'Great balls of fire' (in their version of 'Lucy'), Dion's 'The wanderer' (in 'Fixing a hole'), Elvis Presley's 'His latest flame' (in 'Lovely Rita'), Del Shannon's 'Runaway' (in 'She's leaving home'), and many others. The cleverest pastiche appears on 'Within you without you', which is played in a free jazz style, probably closest to that of Ornette Coleman or Don Cherry from around the early 1960s: from a 1950s American perspective, this would have sounded as outlandish as the orientalism of the original. The opening verses of 'A day in the life' take the chord sequences of Buddy Holly's 'Peggy Sue', while the characteristic catch in Holly's voice is present on the words 'oh boy' (and it was not present in Holly's song of that name!). The first orchestral crescendo is replaced with the simple sounds of a plane flying overhead as the music slows to the central section, which is foisted upon Holly's 'Everyday' (an apt reference to the supposed origin of McCartney's interpolation). The dream sequence pays reference to The Browns' 'Three bells' (a saccharine song about a funeral), while what had been the second orchestral crescendo begins to increase tension by repeating the final harmonic pattern (taken from Holly's 'Heartbeat') up a tone, again beneath the retrieval of the plane sounds. Then, the final held E chord mutates into the sound of a plane crash (at the point at which the 'Heartbeat' motif is suddenly cut short), over which is heard what purports to be a recording of Holly's own death in a plane crash in 1959. Far from the disinterested observer of the crash report that Lennon was in the original, it is now the performer himself who dies (as, of course, did Lennon). Thus, what probably began as yet another slice of cleverness and fun ends up feeling almost profound.

Homages to *Sgt. Pepper* can be still more subtle than this, and probably also unintentional. I shall restrict myself to one example. The wordlessness of the dream sequence of 'A day in the life' is particularly potent: melodic contour, harmonic underpinning and texture were lifted by heavy rock group Deep Purple to create a dream sequence within the song 'Strange kind of woman' (1971). The same contour and sequence appears in the music to the early 1990s UK advertisement for 'only the crumbliest flakiest chocolate', although of course without the wordlessness. In this way a musical sequence can assume a near iconic quality.

From the numbers of people immediately enraptured by *Sgt. Pepper* – whether ordinary listeners, engaged critics or working musicians – the album seems to have spoken (in a way no other has) for its generation, by the direct wish of that generation, through their appropriation of it, rather than through any imposition of it on them. Yet, to note that its songs are not 'as good' as those on *Revolver*, *Rubber Soul* or *Pet Sounds*, for instance, is to suggest that its importance was 'cultural' rather than 'musical'.[22] I find it increasingly difficult to enforce such a separation. 'Musical meanings' inhere not only in musical sounds and their relationships, but are also delineated in their social, theoretical, technological and visual (i.e. cultural) mediations. Thus, the musical object that is *Sgt. Pepper* is more than the sounds of the disc, but its meaning is dependent on those sounds.[23] The album could have been the most cleverly, painstakingly and intricately organized succession of musical sounds (which we know it wasn't); but, had it not been made to do a considerable amount of consequent cultural work, the musical effort which produced it would literally have had no import. It was, and is, musically important in its representation of that generation.

6

Legacy

'Its enormous success was to have unfortunate consequences in succeeding years, when some truly awful "concept" albums in the style of *Pepper* got taken very seriously indeed by people who should have known better.'[1] *Sgt. Pepper* was the high point of a cumulative process which changed the nature of the game that was Anglophone popular music. As I have already suggested, the major available positions in the preceding few years can be summarized in terms of 'pop' (represented, perhaps, by Herman's Hermits or, now, the Monkees) and 'rock' (represented by the Rolling Stones and, subsequently, by Cream or Jimi Hendrix) with the Beatles, despite their rock 'n' roll credentials and the rollicking vocals of which McCartney was capable, tending towards the former.[2] At the time, *Sgt. Pepper* seemed to mark rock music's coming of age, an issue I shall return to at the close of this chapter. Now, of course, with jaded memories, we think of it as ushering in an era of pomposity, with varying degrees of seriousness,[3] to which punk rock formed the inevitable antidote. The case was not clear at the time, for although the entire pop/rock edifice was adding storeys at a remarkable rate, 1967 still supported a very strong 'established' popular music market in the UK, catered to by Engelbert Humperdinck (who prevented 'Penny Lane'/'Strawberry Fields' from reaching No. 1), Petula Clark, Ken Dodd and the like. The distinction between 'rock' and 'pop', and the growing paradigmatic criterion of 'authenticity' (founded on such issues as whether one could have faith in the singer's expressed emotions) was, however, still there. The question after 1967 was whether 'progressive' pop/rock was to be trusted, because it was dealing with issues 'deeper' than simply interpersonal relationships. In the long run, the answer turned out to be 'no' (at least, that is, until a later generation of bands discovered the delight of pastiching the Beatles, of which more later). The debate is concisely captured by comparison of Derek Jewell's support for what was music as performance, rather than music for 'frugging to', as against Nik Cohn's sadness at the Beatles' journey 'far beyond Pop, beyond instinct and pure energy. Limp and self-obsessed [*Sgt. Pepper*] was Art. Not art: Art . . . without pop, without its image and its flash and its myths, they didn't add up to much . . . viewed as Art, they were desperately shorn – glib, simplistic, complacent.'[4]

In MacDonald's reasoned argument, *Sgt. Pepper* marked the zenith of the Beatles' recording career, after which even *Abbey Road* was something of a failure, an argument which tends to elide judgements of aesthetics and inter-personal relations (since Lennon's dislike of McCartney had become apparent to all by this time). Until 1967, there is little disagreement with the view that the Beatles led the field in innovation and, despite the views put forward in chapter 3, *Sgt. Pepper* is often seen as the album in which the rock *auteur* was invented: in particular, *Magical Mystery Tour* and *Let It Be* are disparaged for their lack of authorial control. There is, however, a more charitable interpretation, which acknowledges that the rules of the game had been fundamentally changed in 1967. Having exploited the studio to their maximum capability the Beatles began the process of returning music to its being as process (from whence rock 'n' roll had originally come little over a decade earlier) except that, rather than do this through the, now impossible, live performance, it took place through the somewhat 'formless' (i.e. not song-like) extended jams of which John Lennon's later 'Give peace a chance' seems to me a superb example. That procedure fell out of favour, as we know, when song structures recaptured the ground lost to extended jams and extended pieces by the late 1970s, a position that holds even to this day (although there are isolated signs in bands as diverse as Suede and Verve). The irony lies in the fact that this process was chosen by a band who gave up touring.

Sgt. Pepper, disagreements notwithstanding, is best understood as a concept. This is made particularly clear by some of the ideas surfacing within it – the surest way to maintain a concept is to supply it with a narrative, and one in visual form is more easily assimilated than a thematic one. Indeed, after the album's release on 1 June 1967, *NME* reported on 10 June that a film based on it – an investigation of the persona, called *Shades of Personality* – had been proposed (this came a week before notice of the *Yellow Submarine* film project). Three weeks later, the film had been scrapped (because it would be 'no longer topical by that time', i.e. by its release), to be replaced by *Magical Mystery Tour*.[5] Following the success of the films of *A Hard Day's Night* and *Help!*, both of which constructed a loose narrative around unrelated songs, the potential power of a film was clear. And yet, any film based on *Sgt. Pepper* would necessarily be so complex (and require a great deal of planning) as to make speedy completion impossible, hence the concern about loss of topicality. It docs not appear that anyone involved foresaw that interest in the project would remain even after six months, let alone after three decades. The idea of a 'pop classic', or of writing 'for posterity', was not yet an issue, as we shall see.

If we insist on maintaining a distinction between 'musical' and 'socio-logical' importance, then we must certainly acknowledge that *Sgt. Pepper* was crucial in that second sphere. Harry Shapiro notes that on the album's release, popular awareness of LSD in particular increased dramatically, and that LSD 'brought colour into the lives of many young people, most of whom never touched the stuff. Hippy fashions in ethnic textiles swirled through the streets to the jangle of bells and beads. There were psychedelic films, rock light shows, often unreadable underground newspapers in multi-coloured prints and, of course, the music. Pop co-opted and sanitized acid. The very word "acid" sounded hard and dangerous, a corrosive element in society; "flower-power" on the other hand, was safe and innocuous.'[6] Old rhythm 'n' blues artists (e.g. Graham Bond, whose band nurtured future Cream members Jack Bruce and Ginger Baker) failed to slip into psychedelia as the mods had. In the wake of *Sgt. Pepper*, straightforward rock 'n' roll was banished for some years, although the Beatles themselves would return to it (perhaps in ironical form). The 'concept' album gave rise to others whose album covers imitated art, albums designed to play from beginning to end without a break (except for that necessitated by turning the record over), and even double and triple albums. For the first time, the album market became more lucrative than the singles market, and therein can be found one of the principal reasons for artistic developments.

Hatch and Millward note how far things had come in ten years. No longer was there a desire for separation between 'popular' music and 'art' music, a desire originally symbolized for them by Chuck Berry's 'Roll over Beethoven' and 'Rock and roll music' (both 1957). Instead, in the wake of the Beatles there was a striving for legitimization, for an attempt to appropriate the 'classical' – or at least to show that the two musics could be merged (this was symbolized by McCartney's insistence on the 'influence' of composers like Stockhausen). In practice, this was to take three distinct turns, although I shall suggest a fourth possibility at the conclusion.

The first to arrive was the 'concept' album itself where, rather than a set of tracks without any specific theme, a series of songs would be written all pertaining to a ruling idea. Even here British bands had been preceded, for some would make a similar argument for sides three and four of *Freak Out!*, Frank Zappa and the Mothers of Invention's debut album of late 1966. The Beach Boys' *Pet Sounds* remains a set of unconnected songs, although they share a similarity of tone. The Moody Blues were the first British band to join this particular bandwagon: *Days of Future Passed*, a series of songs structured around different times of day, was released in late 1967, and was followed by *In Search of the Lost Chord* (1968), *On the Threshold of a Dream* and *To our Children's Children's Children* (both 1969). These made explicit the 'message' of (spiritual) fulfilment discernible in *Sgt. Pepper*, but probably through their unsubtlety have failed to retain interest. They would be followed by the more obscure and, thus, probably more successful[7] surreal narratives of Genesis ('Supper's ready' on *Foxtrot* (1972) or the entirety of the double album *The Lamb Lies Down on Broadway* (1974) and the more overt spiritual meanderings of Jon Anderson and Yes (especially *Tales from Topographic Oceans* (1974)). It needs to be remembered that there was no direct equation of 'concept album' and 'progressive rock'. Both the Who's *Tommy* and the Kinks' *Arthur (or the Decline and Fall of the British Empire)* (both 1969) can be described as the former but not the latter.

Although these albums are frequently discussed as though they make use of certain stylistic features of European classicism, this is not the case. Such music forms a second strand of what followed *Sgt. Pepper*, a strand that takes a range of influences; chiefly more 'advanced' harmonies learned from jazz and from late nineteenth-century European concert music, and electronic sounds and studio techniques learned from the European avant garde, especially Stockhausen and Berio. Here the examples are more diffuse, but would include 'Revolution 9' on *The*

Beatles (1968), the arrangement of part of Brahms's Second Symphony on Yes's *Fragile* (1971), Keith Emerson's infatuation with Slavic and Russian musics first with The Nice (1967–9) and subsequently with Emerson, Lake and Palmer (in which he took on board Bartók, Musorgsky, Janáček, and even Parry, Copland and Falla), and King Crimson's avant-garde improvisatory explorations (particularly during the years 1969–74). In this context, Hatch and Millward suggest that most bands adopted the notion of producing work of 'symphonic length' as the surest way to appear progressive.[8] This hides, I think, a common misrepresentation, for even late nineteenth-century symphonic movements (i.e. the length that plays without a break) very rarely exceed fifteen minutes, and certainly do not aim for forty minutes as a norm. As we have seen, as early as June 1967 Bob Dawbarn was noting the recent incursion particularly of 'classical' and 'Indian' musics into pop, in terms of instrumentation, but also of melodic patternings. We even find such an avowed pop band as Dave Dee, Dozy, Beaky, Mick and Tich producing pop pastiches of Greek and Latin 'ethnic' sounds ('Zabadak' and 'Xanadu') as early as 1965. In the case of *Sgt. Pepper*, of course, the incursion of 'classical' (e.g. the strings in 'She's leaving home' or the orchestra in 'A day in the life') required new hands – these were instruments which had to be imported along with their players, and imported through the agency of their producer/arranger. The inability of the working-class band to resist the invitations of the educated musician replays, in a sense, the accommodations black US singers had made with a producer like Phil Spector. Perhaps the issue is less one of striving for legitimacy from below, than of easy annexation from above.

The third strand has aspects in common with both of the previous strands, but is clearly distinguishable: this is the realm of rock opera. Unlike both the above, rock opera needs a consistent narrative (indeed, this is almost all that the word 'opera' means in this context). The first British rock opera (never staged, of course), appears to have been the Pretty Things' *S. F. Sorrow*, released in late 1968. Critically acclaimed (particularly by the burgeoning London underground movement of which, together with Pink Floyd, they are foundational), the album did not sell well. The Who's *Tommy* arrived six months later, and is now almost universally derided for its pretensions (until its 1996 appearance on the London stage, that is). Within a short space of time it was clear that this music had failed to gain the legitimization it had sought and, although concept albums (of some sort or other) would frequently appear to varying degrees of success,[9] by the end of the next decade the 'three-minute single' had again become paramount.

If we require a viable historical model, there is one which will help us understand such shifts, and that is to observe a dialectical relationship between successive turns to sophistication and simplification. Thus, beginning (randomly) from the 1950s, the sophistication apparent in the work of Frank Sinatra encounters the simplification of rock 'n' roll even in some of the early work by the Beatles (their attempt at a song like 'Baby it's you', for example). As we have seen, their own work embodies both the sophistication of 'A day in the life' and the simplification issuing from the *Let it Be* sessions; the sophistication of progressive rock which developed partly out of *Sgt. Pepper* itself met the simplification of mid-1970s punk in the work of a band like Marillion,[10] and so on. It seems to me that such a model is more accurate than any assumed single linear trajectory.

Nevertheless, by 1968 we can witness one crucial development, namely the potential for escape from the pop song as a three-minute little fiction. This raises the issue of 'authorship' which has lain dormant throughout this study so far. A great deal of ordinary thinking about, and listening to, popular music takes place within the assumption that the singer acts as author of the message contained within the song, which is thereby conveyed to the audience. Frequently, this message is assumed to originate within the singer, such that listeners thereby gain privileged access to some normally hidden corner of the singer's private mental/emotional life. Many singers have, of course, traded on the notions of authenticity implied by this perception. Careful thought will normally reveal that the 'persona' generated by the singer is precisely that, a persona generated through various means of artifice (publicity, costume, gesture, expression, and the like). In a series of case studies, David Brackett has recently demolished such a model through a careful discussion of the extent to which the biographical details of the singers Billie Holiday and Hank Williams, in particular, contribute to the affect of their songs. He talks of the possibility (we might even say probability) 'of a *multiplicity* of authorial voices in the musical text'.[11] For the Beatles, of course, the multiplicity of authorial voices is hardly worth remarking on: identification of Lennon's and McCartney's 'voices' is standard, while the 'voices' of Martin, Harrison and Starr are equally present in their musical contributions to the final product. A detailed investigation of even a single verse from this angle would be fruitful, but space precludes such an investigation in this book. Indeed, because such considerations can lead scholars into wanton hermeneutic play, I prefer to approach the question from the exact opposite position: from the assumption that each expression is actually a fiction. I have developed this notion elsewhere,[12] but an outline may be pertinent here. A great deal of critical commentary has always promoted music which seems full of 'feel', is largely improvised, and is by players who are unlikely to be able to expound with any verbal precision the techniques they use. The reason for such critical valorization was, in large part, to demonstrate that the aesthetic criteria of the Central European canon do not have universal validity, but the result was to assume (in ignorance of the operation of musical technique and skill in practising musicians of all kinds) that such music was a vehicle for the direct expression of raw, sub- (or super-) literate, unmediated experience. I believe all such critical attempts to be wishful thinking: in contrast, we must regard the song always as a fiction, both in the sense that no expression of experience is unmediated by some code system or other, and also in the sense that, even where autobiography is the aim, it represents a translation into a foreign medium (i.e. words and other sounds). Indeed, for the era under discussion so far, although audiences may have believed this position (connived at by bands themselves), most bands do not seem to have been prey to self-delusions. This underlies my unease with too literal autobiographical interpretations of even Lennon's songs. Drawn from experience they may be, but they are fictions none the less.

By 1968, the birth of progressive rock was marked by an expressed desire to escape the confines of this fiction produced for entertainment alone. The irony is of course clear, for this desire was not supported by those critics who regarded 'pure' Afro-American forms (the furthest we could get from progressive rock) as the means to unmediated expression. As Chambers notes, 'the "truths" of the individual "artist" replace and refine vaguer populist sentiments . . . [m]usical "authenticity" now suggested a new project, one that was simultaneously "political" and "artistic"'.[13] This was not the first time that such a development had taken place. The most notable instance had been when jazz began to take itself seriously (when swing became bop in the early 1940s) and the audience diminished in turn. An interesting English precursor can be found in the minor controversy over British dance band music in the early 1930s between renowned society bandleader (Bert) Ambrose and Savoy Hotel bandleader Fred Elizalde. Ambrose played very little jazz, and once declared, when playing in Monte Carlo, 'if I couldn't hear the surf, I knew we were playing too loud'.[14] Elizalde's band, although employed for the same types of booking, played jazz (to the acclaim of *Melody Maker*'s critics and readers). In 1929, Elizalde wrote an article for *Gramophone* entitled 'Jazz – what of the future?', which promoted the development of new and interesting rhythms (which could change during the course of a song), getting away from verse and chorus structure, and the suggestion that the role of melody in dance music was really secondary. In other words, he predicted some of the directions jazz would actually explore in the coming decades. The following month, Ambrose replied to *Gramophone* in a letter, suggesting that the predictions were absurd and would never work (his justification being that, if he tried them at the Mayfair, the floor would empty in a minute!). The following month, influential staff writer Edgar Jackson came down on Elizalde's side, pointing out that 'dance records are listened to far more often than they are played for dancing'. Within a few months, however, Elizalde was on the way back to his native Philippines. It appeared, then, that for the British, a music which was fun could not be taken seriously as well.

In the late 1960s, the problem was broadly the same. Critical reaction to what became generically known as 'progressive rock' was, at the least, ambivalent, most grounds for criticism reducing to complaints that a 'fun' music for all had been replaced by a 'serious' music for the few. The term 'progressive', however, has stuck, for certain features held generally in common between the musics mentioned above appeared to warrant the attribution of 'progress'. In the first place, many lyricists attempted to write self-conscious poetry, i.e. containing layers of meaning that were not self-evident (following Lennon's model in 'Lucy' or 'Mr Kite', themselves perhaps pale imitations of Bob Dylan's word-spinning). In the second, there was the use of technology to harness new sounds (although rarely new ways of organizing those sounds) which frequently suggested alternate realities, either of science fiction or of internal space.[15] This moved the music to regions out of the reach of amateur and semi-professional performers, who had neither access to the studio technology involved nor the finances to afford the live equipment required for successful performance. In the third, there was the striving for legitimization which crossed the boundaries of the three-minute song structure, whether or not any stylistic fusion with 'classical' language was attempted. Examples are legion, but among the more noteworthy might be songs like Gentle Giant's 'Knots' (1972), which takes as its starting-point radical psychiatrist R. D. Laing's influential *Knots*, portraying the desperate confusions to which inter-personal (un)relationships so frequently lead, and Jethro Tull's *Thick as a Brick* (1972) or *Passion Play* (1973), both album-length pieces which were critically blasted for their pretensions (notwithstanding the fact that *Passion Play* distinctly falls into ten linked songs, an introduction, coda and fairy tale).

There were, therefore, a number of musico-stylistic features which enabled this flowering of experiment in the late 1960s, giving musicians the kind of creative freedom now restricted to very few 'difficult' artists, such as Kate Bush. In order to understand it more fully, however, we have to take account of more general factors.[16] The late 1960s and early 1970s inhabited an extraordinarily unified social/economic climate without which such developments, however artistically 'necessary', could not have taken place. The first of these is the arena of technological change. By 1967 such advances, combined with a change of attitude at live gigs (where performers were now to be seen as much as heard, and were valued for their images rather than their products), meant that the studio rather than the stage was beginning to act as a focus for musical activity. (We have seen the origins of this in the experiences of the Beatles, although it can certainly be traced back through the work of producers like Joe Meek and Phil Spector.) This change of attitude corresponds to a divergence of listening practices: at large festivals (such as Monterey, Woodstock or the Isle of Wight) or in privacy, rather than in clubs and small venues. The greater investments in time and money that this required meant that it was economic to work on albums rather than singles, so that albums began to replace singles as the focus for musicians. A change was thereby signalled in the use of music by both its originators and its consumers.

Secondly, the greater sophistication that studios were permitted through technological developments became coupled with the demand for political and social 'radicalism' inherent in the protest movement, and which found its strongest expression in the Paris riots of May 1968 and the more widespread anger at US involvement in Indo-China.[17] These twin features enabled musicians to inhabit an ideology of self-expression, with a freedom from the constraints of a dancing audience who required their investment to pay off with immediate (somatic) returns. The musicians' ideology thus became integrated into the new youth ideology where 'doing your own thing' became the operative phrase. (Ironically, of course, this very idea became hijacked by punk's 'do it yourself', where it was utilized to very different artistic, but perhaps not very different social, ends.) This move towards longer-term gratification pleased the major record labels, for the term and product 'progressive' (which itself connotes concern with aesthetic rather than with immediate qualities) helped them to differentiate the new product from 'commercial' pop (also, of course, a product under their control), and to service the very fast growing student market with a whole series of 'separate' 'progressive' labels (that these were wholly owned by the majors was often not apparent). The ultimate falsity of this position became clear when CBS coined the slogan 'The revolutionaries are all on CBS'. In the early days, many bands, particularly in San Francisco's burgeoning counter-culture, did not even have recording contracts.[18] Here, as had been the case in Liverpool seven years earlier, accessibility of bands for their immediate audiences had been very important; both players and listeners were from the same generation and the same neighbourhoods.

The role of the Beatles in this development was crucial not only through their utilization of the studio as a working tool in its own right (as evidenced in *Sgt. Pepper*), but in their being the band who helped to spread British rock from its working-class roots (the audiences in the Cavern and other Liverpool clubs) to a college and university base (at a time when access to higher education was increasing) and the speedy development of the college circuit which labels turned to their advantage. However, none of this would have been possible were it not for economic circumstances: Frith makes the point that 'the worldwide impact of the Beatles can now be seen to have been an extraordinary and unrepeatable business event'. Marwick points out that the average weekly earnings of adult men rose by 34 per cent between 1955 and 1960, and by 130 per cent between 1955 and 1967, a growth matched by the average earnings of the salaried bourgeoisie (having taken inflation into account). Although the prices of necessities continued to rise through this period, the prices of the products of Wilson's 'white heat of technological revolution' (television sets and record players, washing machines and vacuum cleaners) were actually falling, giving rise to the, subsequently squandered, economic boom of the mid-1960s.[19] This meant that labels could afford to 'invest' in artists, giving them for a short while a freedom to experiment, and even allowing limited control over the product and its marketing.

The Beatles officially disbanded in 1970. With the exception of the loving parodies by BBC-TV offshoot The Rutles (1978), their image went into unsurprising decline such that, like other early 1960s 'pop' bands (the Kinks and the Who being notable exceptions), their recordings were viciously parodied within the new wave and punk movements (think only of the Flying Lizards' utterly exploitative 1980 version of the Beatles' own cover 'Money'). Over subsequent years, however, their music has been rehabilitated to the extent that the CD reissue of *Sgt. Pepper* reached No. 1, twenty years after the original (some of these sales, at least, being to first-time purchasers), while the two double-CD *Anthology* albums' combined sales in 1995 exceeded sales of any of the original albums.[20] In addition, more benign, and even flattering, pastiches have begun to surface. Note the songs on XTC's *Skylarking* (1986); the cunning musical references to 'All you need is love', 'I am the walrus' and 'Hello Goodbye' on Tears for Fears' 'Sowing the seeds of love' (1989); the rediscovery of (what for a long while was hackneyed) guitar phasing for The Stone Roses' 'Waterfall' (1989); and more recently a whole host of references: the Boo Radleys' *Wake up!* (1995) is typical. Much of this comes as part of the renascent psychedelia, in tandem with rave culture and, indeed, in late 1995 the media were heavily reinventing the old battle between the Beatles and the Rolling Stones, now recast as Essex's Blur and Manchester's Oasis (although in the wake of their success in the Brit Awards 1996, Oasis were being hailed in the *Los Angeles Times* as 'what the Beatles might have sounded like today')! With this, finally, the aura which has surrounded the Beatles for so long has diminished to the level of any other band so that we can see how truly intrinsic to its generation *Sgt. Pepper* was.

The chief legacy of *Sgt. Pepper* is, then, one of a failed striving for legitimacy, now sufficiently far distant to be looked on with benign, amused forbearance. In conclusion, however, there is quite another perspective to be taken on the album which may be more particularly relevant to the immediate context for this book. Without for a moment accepting the assertion that twentieth-century popular music's utilization of tonal materials makes it the natural inheritor of our Central European musical past (of territory abdicated by musical modernism), its very use of those materials does suggest that larger milieu.

It is quite possible to see the continuities of *Sgt. Pepper* in terms of territory familiar from nineteenth-century Austrian and German song-cycles. Take Schumann's *Dichterliebe*, for instance: a series of songs sharing tone and substance, but without a narrative thread, and where the recall at the end of the final (sixteenth) song of the postlude to the twelfth song functions in a manner analogous to that of the reprise of 'Sgt. Pepper's Lonely Hearts Club Band'. *Sgt. Pepper* does not maintain an equivalent key argument, although the presence of V–I structures ('With a little help'/'Lucy', 'Getting better'/'Fixing a hole') and shared tonics ('Within you'/'When I'm sixty-four', 'Lovely Rita'/'Good morning') might suggest a similar reading.

Alternatively, the generic way the album is set out, with its rousing opening, its big ending, its whimsical interlude, its slow number, its earnest mid-point, finds echoes in other contemporary offerings – King Crimson's *In the Court of the Crimson King* (1969), Yes's *Fragile*, Jethro Tull's *Aqualung*, Led Zeppelin's *IV* (all 1971) and Emerson Lake and Palmer's *Trilogy* (1972) come immediately to mind – suggesting a possible line of interpretation related to that of the nineteenth-century 'multi-piece'.[21] There are few overt motivic references, of course, although the appearance of prominent lower descending lines (see Exx. 4.3, 4.5, 4.6, 4.14), fifth-cycles (Exx. 4.1, 4.2, 4.5, 4.8, 4.9, 4.11, 4.12, 4.13) and both rising (Exx. 4.1, 4.9) and falling (Exx. 4.2, 4.3, 4.7, 4.8, 4.11, 4.12, 4.13, 4.14) structural lines (combined in Exx. 4.4 and 4.6) lends credence to such a view.

Then again, 'A day in the life' might be seen as yet another solution to the nineteenth century's problem of ending the large-scale work. The problem was most clearly stated by Beethoven's Ninth Symphony, of course, and even that finale's *reculer pour mieux sauter* has its counterpart here. The reprise of 'Sgt. Pepper' gathers together all that preceded it (as in Middleton's interpretation), while the final song (the new direction) doesn't have the manners to wait until its predecessor is ended (»*laßt uns angenehmere anstimmen*« indeed!).

And so, with these intentionally vague pointers towards a whole new contextualization, it seems to me that *Sgt. Pepper* will, indeed, grow to command that space between Schoenberg and his voice and, in so doing, will confirm the damming of that mainstream, marking the paradigmatic shift towards a more flexible, less guilt-ridden appropriation and utilization of musical materials.

Appendix

	Recording sessions	Final mono mix
Sgt. Pepper	4 days; 1 Feb 1967– 6 March 1967	6 March 1967
With a little help	2 days; 29–30 March 1967	31 March 1967
Lucy in the sky	2 days; 1–2 March 1967	3 March 1967
Getting better	4 days; 9–23 March 1967	23 March 1967
Fixing a hole	2 days; 9–21 Feb 1967	21 Feb 1967
She's leaving home	2 days; 17–20 March 1967	20 March 1967
Being for the benefit	5 days; 17 Feb–31 March 1967	31 March 1967
Within you without you	3 days; 15 March–3 April 1967	4 April 1967
When I'm sixty-four	4 days; 6–21 Dec 1966	30 Dec 1966
Lovely Rita	4 days; 23 Feb–21 March 1967	21 March 1967
Good morning	5 days; 8 Feb–29 March 1967	19 April 1967
Sgt. Pepper (reprise)	1 day; 1 April 1967	1 April 1967
A day in the life	5 days; 19 Jan–22 Feb 1967	22 Feb 1967
(Playout groove)	1 day; 21 April 1967	21 April 1967
Strawberry Fields	7 days; 24 Nov–21 Dec 1966	22 Dec 1966
Penny Lane	9 days; 29 Dec 1966–17 Jan 1967	25 Jan 1967
It's only a northern song	3 days; 13–20 Feb 1967	21 April 1967

Source: Lewisohn, *Beatles Recording Sessions*

Notes

Preface

1 Wilfrid Mellers, 'Lonely beat', *New Statesman* (2 June 1967), 770–1; Mellers, *Twilight of the Gods*, 82–104; Jonathan Dunsby, *Schoenberg: Pierrot Lunaire* (Cambridge: Cambridge University Press, 1992), 74.
2 Lewisohn, *The Beatles Recording Sessions*; Hertsgaard, *A Day in the Life*.

1 Inheritance

1 See Raymond Williams, *Culture and Society 1780–1950* (London: Penguin, 1963); Stuart Hall and Paddy Whannel (eds.), *The Popular Arts* (London: Hutchinson, 1964); Stuart Hall and Tony Jefferson, *Resistance Through Rituals* (London: Hutchinson, 1976). Two commentaries are particularly valuable: Andrew Milner, *An Introduction to Contemporary Cultural Theory* (London: University College London Press, 1993), chapter 2; and John Storey, *Cultural Theory and Popular Culture* (Hemel Hempstead: Harvester Wheatsheaf, 1993), chapter 3.
2 Quotation from Middleton, *Studying Popular Music*, 14. The 'art theory' reference is particularly indebted to Clement Greenberg's 1939 essay 'Avant garde and kitsch', reprinted in *Art and Culture: Critical Essays* (Boston: Beacon, 1965), 3–21. Other references are to Georgina Born, *Rationalizing Culture* (Berkeley: California University Press, 1995), 45, and Dave Harker, *One for the Money*, 92.
3 For the opposition between cultures, see Milner, *Introduction*, 26–41; Frith, *Sound Effects*, 41–8; and Chambers, *Urban Rhythms*, 15. For the growth of media, see particularly Michael Chanan, *Musica Practica* (London: Verso, 1994), 222; and Simon Frith, 'The Industrialization of Music' and 'The pleasures of the hearth', in *Music for Pleasure* (Cambridge: Polity, 1988), 11–23 and 24–44.
4 The report is Mark Abrams, *The Teenage Consumer* (London: Press Exchange, 1959), 5–10, cited in Harker, *One for the Money*, 74. See also

Marwick, *British Society*, 128 and 135–6. On the relationship between residual, dominant and emergent cultural practices, see Raymond Williams,
Culture (London: Fontana, 1981), 203–5.

5 This move can be very sharply outlined from the swing bands of Ellington and
Basie, with their massed horns, through the 'chamber' bands of Basie to the
jump jazz of Louis Jordan, and thence to Bill Haley's early band and Elvis
Presley's original trio. With the big bands, individual soloists still performed
as part of someone else's band, unlike Haley or Presley. It is not, however, until
the arrival of the Beatles, the Who and the Rolling Stones that band members
are permitted individual identities. For the 'delicious danger' see Chambers,
Urban Rhythms, 22–3 and 33. The Bradley quote is from Dick Bradley,
Understanding Rock'n'Roll (Buckingham: Open University Press, 1992), 84.

6 Richard A. Peterson, 'Why 1955? Explaining the advent of rock music',
Popular Music 9/1 (1990), 105, 113–14.

7 Everett, *You'll Never be Sixteen Again*, 25.

2 Preparation

1 Hertsgaard, *A Day in the Life*, 43.

2 Bob Brunning, *Blues: The British Connection* (Poole: Blandford, 1986),
12–25. For the general importance of the British art school scene to the
development of pop, see Simon Frith and Howard Horne, *Art into Pop*
(London: Methuen, 1987).

3 Many of these are cited by the 'fifth' Beatle, producer George Martin
(*Summer of Love*, 45). There is, of course, a chasm between declaration of an
influence and its analytical incorporation. I tend to endorse the more general-
ized attempts at the latter to which I subsequently refer.

4 Aside from the all-original *A Hard Day's Night*, the Beatles' first five albums
included twenty-four covers: three rhythm 'n' blues numbers, seven rock 'n'
roll, five rockabilly/country and western, four girl group (harmony vocals),
plus single examples of soul, doowop, Broadway show, UK film and the
excruciating 'Mr Moonlight'.

5 Chambers, *Urban Rhythms*, 63. The pair of terms *intensional* and *extensional*
were proposed in Chester, 'Second thoughts', to essentialize the distinction
between rock/pop music (whose structures were formulaic, but where the
interest lay in the subtleties of melodic/rhythmic articulation) and the 'classical' tradition (where that articulation was reckoned more standardized, but
where structures were infinitely malleable).

6 Arnold Shaw, *The Rock Revolution* (London: Collier-MacMillan, 1969),
95–107.

7 Michael Haralambos, *Right On: From Blues to Soul in Black America* (London: Eddison), 1974.

8 Gabree, 'The Beatles in perspective'.

9 The flavour of this position can be gleaned from the articles gathered in section 4 of Hanif Kureishi and Jon Savage (eds.), *The Faber Book of Pop* (London: Faber, 1995). Quotations in this paragraph from Green, *Days in the Life*, 91 and 125; and Christopher Booker, *The Neophiliacs* (London: Fontana, 1970), 235.

10 George Melly, *Revolt into Style* (Oxford: Oxford University Press, 1989), 168ff.; Wicke, *Rock Music*, 76–7; Paul Weller, 'The total look', in Tony Stewart (ed.), *Cool Cats* (London: Eel Pie, 1981), 34; Harry Shapiro, *Waiting for the Man* (London: Mandarin, 1990), 108, 115; and Stanley Cohen, *Folk Devils and Moral Panics* (Oxford: Blackwell, 1990), 189ff.

11 MacDonald, *Revolution in the Head*, 173.

12 Moore, *Rock*, 62–3.

13 Joan Peyser, 'The music of sound or the Beatles and the beatless', in Jonathan Eisen (ed.), *The Age of Rock* (New York: Vintage, 1969), 134; and Middleton, *Pop Music*, 167.

14 Geoffrey Giuliano, *Paint it Black* (London: Virgin, 1994), 13; John Platt, *London's Rock Routes* (London: Fourth Estate, 1985), 37–8; Dick Heckstall-Smith, *The Safest Place in the World* (London: Quartet, 1989), 40; Gary Schofield, *Jagger* (London: Methuen, 1983), 21–2.

15 The confusions of gender within rock have recently been given excellent treatment in Simon Reynolds and Joy Press, *The Sex Revolts* (London: Serpent's Tail, 1995).

16 Note the high pitch on 'that's the end *of* little girl', which effectively punctuates Lennon's anger.

17 Again we must beware of the dangers of an essentialist interpretation: the Stones rhythm 'n' blues base moved into soul and even some (perhaps ill-advised) excursions into pop, even at this period.

18 For the Rolling Stones connection, see Jon Savage, *The Kinks* (London: Faber, 1984). A 'riff' is a simple, repeated fragment of melody, frequently susceptible (without transposition) to harmonization by I, IV and V (at least).

19 Melly, *Revolt into Style*, 79.

20 Mainstream songwriters such as Burt Bacharach, whose material was covered by solo singers such as Sandie Shaw, Dusty Springfield, Tom Jones and Cilla Black, were very familiar with chromatic formulations.

21 Moore, *Rock*, 89–91.

22 A full discussion of the development of music radio in the UK can be found

in Stephen Barnard, *On the Radio* (Buckingham: Open University Press, 1989). The information on Radio Caroline appears in Harker, *One for the Money*, 79.

3 Inception

1 As an aid to the following discussion, the Appendix lays out the album's tracks, together with dates of recording, taken from Lewisohn, *The Beatles Recording Sessions*.
2 Alan Walsh, 'The answer facing pop', *Melody Maker* (20 May 1967).
3 This qualification is due to early American releases being cobbled-together versions of British albums.
4 Mann, 'The Beatles revive hopes', 92; and Dawbarn, 'When does pop become art?'.
5 On this and many of the subsequent sources given in this chapter, I rely on Turner, *A Hard Day's Write*, 117–34.
6 Taylor, *It Was Twenty Years Ago*, 28, 192; MacDonald, *Revolution in the Head*, 178; Hertsgaard, *A Day in the Life*, 7; Mellers, 'Lonely beat', 771.
7 Martin, *Summer of Love*, 120.
8 MacDonald, *Revolution in the Head*, 191. The McCartney interview is in Alan Aldridge, 'The Beatles not all that turned on', in Jonathan Eisen (ed.), *The Age of Rock* (New York: Vintage, 1969), 143.
9 This phrase is taken from William Johnston, *Silent Music: The Art of Meditation* (London: Fontana-Collins, 1974), 80–1, where it is used in Zen to mean to pass on to others the understanding gained through such rarefied experiences.
10 Norrie Drummond, Review of *Sgt. Pepper*, *New Musical Express* (27 May 1967).
11 Charlie Gillett's monumental history follows Lennon in insisting that many of the songs were rather casually put together, implying mediocrity. See Gillett, *The Sound of the City* (London: Souvenir, 1983), 267.
12 See Martin, *Summer of Love*, 65; and Allen Evans, Preview of *Sgt. Pepper*, *New Musical Express*, (20 May 1967).
13 MacDonald, *Revolution in the Head*, 197, Martin, *Summer of Love*, 148–50.
14 Martin, *Summer of Love*, 6.

4 Commentary

1 I have no intention here of rehearsing those well-trodden arguments over the 'ultimate' significance of any aspect of such an 'ephemeral' genre. My

'significant others' are MacDonald, *Revolution in the Head*; Mellers, *Twilight of the Gods*; Middleton, *Pop Music;* and Riley, *Tell Me Why*.

2 Middleton, *Studying Popular Music,* discusses the concepts of 'under-coding' and 'over-coding'. Broadly, an 'over-coded' work over-determines its range of possible meanings, while an 'under-coded' work does the opposite. Moore, 'U2 and the myth' develops the concept of *affordance* in the interpretation of popular music.

3 Alan F. Chalmers, *Science and its Fabrication* (Buckingham: Open University Press, 1990).

4 Moore, 'The so-called "Flattened seventh" in rock', 185–7; and Allen Forte, *The American Popular Ballad in the Golden Era, 1924–1950* (Princeton: Princeton University Press, 1995). The most recent example of the strict Schenkerian approach is probably Walter Everett's reduction of the entire second side of the Beatles' *Abbey Road* to an *Ursatz*. See Everett, 'The Beatles as composers', especially example 7 (224).

5 Note that, in a style like this, the 4/4 'bar' is defined by the strong presence of (normally) the snare drum on the 'backbeat', i.e. on beats 2 and 4 of the bar.

6 See Moore, 'Patterns of harmony', 86–7, 90–1. The mixolydian mode has a flattened seventh degree with respect to the major scale: the harmonic modality of rock is outlined in Moore, *Rock*, 48–50.

7 Although it was heard as James Brown by an early reviewer: Chris Welch, 'Now let boring controversy begin', *Melody Maker* (3 June 1967).

8 Throughout this chapter, references to MacDonald, Mellers, Middleton and Riley will not be specifically acknowledged, other than through note 1 (above).

9 Clayson, *Ringo Starr*, 114, 115.

10 The Leslie speaker revolves in its cabinet, creating a constant wavering sense of spatial dislocation, but lack of movement.

11 Derek Jewell's review of *Sgt. Pepper*, *Sunday Times* (4 June 1967); Jack Kroll's review 'It's getting better', *Newsweek*, (26 June 1967), 70; Richard Goldstein's review in the *New York Times* (18 June 1967); and Mellers, *Twilight of the Gods*, 89; Riley, *Tell Me Why*, 215; Whiteley, *The Space Between the Notes*, 42–60; Middleton, *Pop Music*, 244; and MacDonald, *Revolution in the Head*, 191.

12 MacDonald, *Revolution in the Head*, 192.

13 Everett, 'Text-painting'.

14 After all, phrase extensions and contractions are pretty frequent within rock. See Moore, *Rock*, 40–1.

15 Martin, *Summer of Love*, 91–2.

16 Riley, *Tell Me Why*, 220.

17 Lewisohn, *The Beatles Recording Sessions*, 86–7.
18 MacDonald, *Revolution in the Head*, 178.
19 This is described in Bonnie C. Wade, *Music in India: the Classical Traditions* (New Delhi: Manohar, 1994), 185–6.
20 Peyser, 'The music of sound', 132.
21 How far ahead might be estimated by Oasis's recent utilization of the same device – using a song which can be appropriated by an older generation – on their 1995 album *(What's the Story) Morning Glory*. The song in question is 'She's electric'. My thanks to Dai Griffiths for reminding me of this.
22 According to MacDonald, *Revolution in the Head*, 189–90.
23 Mellers is not alone in interpreting the final verse as having learnt from the easy interpolation.
24 The informed reader will realize that this is not the first time I have deviated from Schenkerian orthodoxy's interpretation of parallel surfaces with parallel middleground motions. One of the things that makes rock's strophic forms distinctive, it seems to me, is the very possibility of such reinterpretations which themselves can give meaning to a succession of strophes.
25 Richard Goldstein, *The Poetry of Rock* (New York: Bantam, 1969), 131–2; Middleton, *Pop Music*, 234; MacDonald, *Revolution in the Head*, 181; and Martin, *Summer of Love*, 148.
26 MacDonald, *Revolution in the Head*, 181 and Middleton, *Pop Music*, 245. As an aside, it is interesting how offhand remarks enter the mythology, viz. the oft-referred-to 'Wagnerian episode'. This is not actually the crescendi (which McCartney would rather refer to Stockhausen *et al.*, as we would expect), but the four bass notes immediately prior to 3′ 19″ and the final verse. Goldstein, the first to use the analogy, terms them a 'Wagnerian descent', whence they become Poirier's 'Wagnerian episode' ('Learning from the Beatles', 112) and the analogy becomes common stock.
27 Riley, *Tell Me Why*, 218. These layers of uncertain realities are crucial to the insistence by some cultural theorists of the advent of the 'postmodern'; specifically, here, the notion of the simulacrum developed by Jean Baudrillard, *Simulacra and Simulations* (New York: Semiotext(e), 1983).
28 In *Studying Popular Music*, Middleton talks of the 'under-coding' more common in classical music, where an unambiguous 'meaning' is not to be found (173).
29 Tom Phillips, Review of *Sgt. Pepper*, *Village Voice* (22 June 1967).
30 See Harker, *One for the Money*, 35. *Sgt. Pepper* figures cited from *New Musical Express* (22 April 1967).

5 Reception

1 Note that Mellers was teaching his pre-release copy to his music undergraduates at the University of York, a cohort which contained a number of now-influential musicians and musicologists.

2 Christgau, 'Symbolic comrades', 227.

3 MacDonald, *Revolution in the Head*, 198; Taylor, *It Was Twenty Years Ago*, 24; Stokes, 'The sixties', 370, 371, Mann, 'The Beatles revive hopes', 93; Poirier, 'Learning from the Beatles', 125; Hertsgaard, *A Day in the Life*, 213; and Greil Marcus, *Mystery Train* (London: Omnibus, 1977), 50.

4 Melly, *Revolt into Style*, 126.

5 Pichaske, 'Sustained performances', 59–60; and Poirier, 'Learning from the Beatles', 121–2.

6 Whiteley, *The Space*, 44, 43; and Shapiro, *Waiting for the Man*, 145–6.

7 Whiteley, *The Space*, 40.

8 Drummond's review in *New Musical Express*; Green, *Days in the Life*, 191, Whiteley, *The Space*, 60, 151; and Harker, *One for the Money*, 35. 'SWP' refers to the Socialist Workers' Party, a British radical socialist party with quite a large membership among academics (though not among the general populace), well known for the forthright expression of its views in academic debate.

9 Peyser, 'The music of sound', 132; Riley, *Tell Me Why*, 204; and Kroll, 'It's getting better', 70.

10 Goldstein, *The Poetry of Rock*.

11 Mellers, *Twilight of the Gods*, 188 and 'Lonely beat', 771.

12 Welch, 'Now let boring controversy begin'; Kroll, 'It's getting better'; Poirier, 'Learning from the Beatles', 118; Gabree, 'The Beatles in perspective', 137, Middleton, *Pop Music*, 243; and Whiteley, *The Space Between the Notes*, 40.

13 Hatch and Millward, *From Blues to Rock*, 147; Jewell, Review in the *Sunday Times*, (4 June 1967), 23; Welch, 'Now let boring controversy begin', 5.

14 It is this emphasis on metonymy which distinguishes their 'observational' approach from the metaphor of Bob Dylan's early work (and, more generally, from the introverted singer-songwriter). See David Lodge, *The Modes of Modern Writing* (London: Edward Arnold, 1977), especially 73–81.

15 Poirier, 'Learning from the Beatles', 121; and Kroll, 'It's getting better', 70. My thanks to Dai Griffiths for suggesting the 'northern' line of enquiry.

16 Kroll, 'It's getting better'; Mann, 'The Beatles revive'; Evans, Preview in *New Musical Express* (20 May 1967); in *Village Voice* (22 June 1967). Phillips, Review, 5.

17 Clayson, *Ringo Starr*, 114. This claim is followed by Whiteley, *The Space Between the Notes*, 42.
18 Taylor, *It was Twenty Years Ago*, 24; Martin, *Summer of Love*, 149; Gabree, 'The Beatles in perspective', 135; Stokes, 'The sixties', 370. Perhaps Middleton's persuasive interpretations should simply be counted the most careful of these exegeses.
19 Middleton, *Studying Popular Music*, 173.
20 This is briefly explored in Middleton, *Studying Popular Music*, 198.
21 This may have been partly due to all proceeds going to the charity 'Child-Line'.
22 Mick Houghton writes that '*Revolver* stands as the most timeless and unblemished [Beatles] album . . . it may have been less far reaching in its impact than *Sergeant Pepper*, but it has aged so much more gracefully': 'British beat', in John Collis (ed.), *The Rock Primer* (London: Penguin, 1980), 158. Alan Clayson notes that 'however much its content has been devalued by reassessment, this syncretic work was, technically, an improvement on the preceding LP, *Revolver* . . .': *Ringo Starr*, 113.
23 This position avoids both the positivist recourse to a notion of transcendent aesthetic value, and the sociological reductionism which equates aesthetic value with commercial success, or something similar. See Born, *Rationalizing Culture*, 23; and Lucy Green, *Music on Deaf Ears* (Manchester: Manchester University Press, 1988), particularly 12–37.

6 Legacy

1 Martin, *Summer of Love*, 157.
2 Other positions existed, particularly in the USA (the folk/country-rock of the Byrds, the soul/funk of James Brown and Sly Stone, the underground scene represented by the Velvet Underground), but none of these was yet open to UK bands.
3 Just consider, at either extreme, Slade and Yes.
4 Jewell, Review in the *Sunday Times*, (4 June 1967); Cohn, *A Wop*, 138, 145.
5 Reported in *New Musical Express* (1 July 1967), 8, and *Melody Maker* (9 September 1967), 7.
6 Shapiro, *Waiting for the Man*, 145–6.
7 See Moore, *Rock*, 100, for discussion of the reasons for the valorization of obscurity in such styles.
8 Hatch and Millward, *From Blues to Rock*, 153.
9 One of the most recent at the time of writing was David Bowie's angst-ridden millennial *1. Outside*, from late 1995. Bowie's licence is, of course, legendary.

10 Moore, *Rock*, 127–8.
11 Brackett, *Interpreting Popular Music* (Cambridge: Cambridge University Press, 1995), 15. Many writers tie such a concept into the post-structuralism of Roland Barthes' proclamation of the death of the author ('The death of the author', in *Image-Music-Text*, trans. Stephen Heath (London: Fontana/Collins, 1977), 142–8) or Mikhail Bakhtin's concepts of *dialogism* in the novel, where 'every thought of a character is internally dialogic, adorned with polemic, filled with struggle, or on the contrary is open to inspiration from outside itself', and where the demonstrable presence of such a dialogism is regarded as a criterion of high quality. (*Problems of Dostoevsky's Poetics*, ed. and trans. Caryl Emmerson (Manchester: Manchester University Press, 1984), 293.
12 Moore, *Rock*, 82–6.
13 Chambers, *Urban Rhythms*, 88. Even the concept of 'Afro-American' forms is not without grave problems. See Philip Tagg, 'Open letter: "Black music", "Afro-American music" and "European music"'', *Popular Music* 8/3 (1989), 285–96.
14 Mark Hustwitt, 'Caught in a whirlpool of aching sound: the production of dance music in the 1920s', *Popular Music* 3 (1983), 7–31.
15 Moore, *Rock*, 98–100; Andy Mackay, *Electronic Music* (Oxford: Phaidon, 1981), 86–91.
16 The difficulty in so doing is epitomized in Simon Frith's excellent *Sound Effects*, where he seems unable to decide whether the shift towards rock is primarily enabled by technological (144) or specifically musico-stylistic (150) developments.
17 Steve Jones, *Rock Formation* (Newbury Park, CA: Sage, 1992), 156–83; Michael Chanan, *Repeated Takes* (London: Verso, 1995), 141–8; Robin Denselow (*When the Music's Over*, London: Faber, 1989), 63–85, 92–103.
18 Taylor, *It Was Twenty Years Ago*, 56–61.
19 Frith, *Sound Effects*, 144; Marwick, *British Society*, 118.
20 Figures given in *The Observer* (21 April 1996).
21 Jonathan Dunsby, 'The multi-piece in Brahms: *Fantasien*, op. 116', in Robert Pascall (ed.), *Brahms, Biographical, Documentary and Analytical Studies* (Cambridge: Cambridge University Press, 1983). My gratitude to Dai Griffiths for suggesting this whole, untapped, line of enquiry.

Select bibliography

Chambers, Iain, *Urban Rhythms* (Basingstoke: Macmillan, 1985)

Chester, Andrew, 'Second thoughts on a rock aesthetic: the band', *New Left Review* 62 (1970), 75–82

Christgau, Robert, 'Symbolic comrades', in *The Lennon Companion*, ed. Elizabeth Thomson and David Gutman (Basingstoke: Macmillan, 1981), 226–31

Clayson, Alan, *Ringo Starr: Rich Man or Joker?* (London: Sidgwick & Jackson, 1991)

Cohn, Nik, *A Wop Bop A Loo Bop A Lop Bam Boom* (London: Paladin, 1970)

Davies, Hunter, *The Beatles* (London: Cape, 1985; originally 1968)

Dawbarn, Bob, 'When does pop become art?' *Melody Maker*, 10 June 1967

Everett, Peter, *You'll Never be Sixteen Again* (London: BBC Publications, 1986)

Everett, Walter, 'Text-painting in the foreground and middleground of Paul McCartney's Beatle song 'She's leaving home': a musical study of psychological conflict', *In Theory Only* 9 (1985), 5–13

'The Beatles as composers: the genesis of *Abbey Road*, Side Two', in *Concert Music, Rock, and Jazz since 1945*, ed. Elizabeth West Marvin and Richard Herrmann (Rochester NY: Rochester University Press, 1995), 172–228

Frith, Simon, *Sound Effects* (London: Constable, 1983)

Gabree, John, 'The Beatles in perspective' (1967), reprinted in *The Beatles Reader*, ed. Charles Neises (Ann Arbor: Popular Culture Ink. [*sic*], 1991), 131–8

Green, Jonathon, *Days in the Life* (London: Minerva, 1989)

Harker, Dave, *One for the Money* (London: Hutchinson, 1980)

Hatch, David and Stephen Millward, *From Blues to Rock* (Manchester: Manchester University Press, 1987)

Hertsgaard, Mark, *A Day in the Life* (Basingstoke: Macmillan, 1995)

Lewisohn, Mark, *The Beatles Recording Sessions* (London: Hamlyn/EMI, 1989)

MacDonald, Ian, *Revolution in the Head* (London: Pimlico, 1995)

Mann, William, 'The Beatles revive hopes of progress in pop music', *The Times*,

29 May 1967, reprinted in *The Lennon Companion*, ed. Elizabeth Thomson and David Gutman (Basingstoke: Macmillan, 1981), 89–93

Martin, George, (with William Pearson), *Summer of Love* (London: Pan, 1995)

Marwick, Arthur, *British Society Since 1945* (London: Pelican, 1982)

Mellers, Wilfrid, *Twilight of the Gods: The Beatles in Retrospect* (London: Faber & Faber, 1973)

Middleton, Richard, *Pop Music and the Blues* (London: Gollancz, 1972)
  Studying Popular Music (Buckingham: Open University Press, 1990)

Moore, Allan F., 'Patterns of harmony', *Popular Music* 11/1 (1992), 73–106
  Rock: The Primary Text (Buckingham: Open University Press, 1993)
  'The so-called "flattened seventh" in rock', *Popular Music* 14/2 (1995), 185–201
  'U2 and the myth of authenticity in rock', *Popular Musicology* 3 (1997) forthcoming

Pichaske, David R., 'Sustained performances: "Sgt. Pepper's Lonely Hearts Club Band"' (1972), in *The Beatles Reader* (Ann Arbor: Popular Culture Ink. [*sic*], 1991), 59–62

Poirier, Richard, 'Learning from the Beatles' (1971), in *The Beatles Reader* (Ann Arbor: Popular Culture Ink. [sic], 1991), 107–28

Riley, Tim, *Tell Me Why* (Oxford: Bodley Head, 1988)

Stokes, Geoffrey, 'The sixties', in Ed Ward, Geoffrey Stokes and Ken Tucker, *Rock of Ages* (London: Penguin, 1987), 249–463

Taylor, Derek, *It Was Twenty Years Ago Today* (London: Bantam, 1987)

Turner, Steve, *A Hard Day's Write* (London: Carlton, 1994)

Whiteley, Sheila, *The Space Between the Notes* (London: Routledge, 1992)

Wicke, Peter, *Rock Music: Culture, Aesthetics and Sociology* (Cambridge: Cambridge University Press, 1990)

Discography

Beach Boys, The, *Pet Sounds*, Capitol, 1966.

Beatles, The, *Please Please Me*, Parlophone, 1963 (CD reissue 1987).

Beatles, The, *With The Beatles*, Parlophone, 1963 (CD reissue 1987).

Beatles, The, *A Hard Day's Night*, Parlophone, 1964 (CD reissue 1987).

Beatles, The, *Beatles For Sale*, Parlophone, 1964 (CD reissue 1987).

Beatles, The, *Help!*, Parlophone, 1965 (CD reissue 1987).

Beatles, The, *Rubber Soul*, Parlophone, 1965 (CD reissue 1987).

Beatles, The, *Revolver*, Parlophone, 1966 (CD reissue 1987).

Beatles, The, 'Strawberry Fields Forever/Penny Lane', Parlophone, 1967.

Beatles, The, *Sgt. Pepper's Lonely Hearts Club Band*, Parlophone, 1967 (CD reissue 1987).

Beatles, The, *Magical Mystery Tour*, Parlophone, 1967.

Beatles, The, *The Beatles*, Apple, 1968 (CD reissue 1987).

Beatles, The, *Abbey Road*, Apple, 1969 (CD reissue 1987).

Beatles, The, *Let It Be*, Apple, 1970 (CD reissue 1987).

Beatles, The, *Anthology 2*, Apple, 1995.

Big Daddy, *Sgt. Pepper's Lonely Hearts Club Band*, Rhino, 1992.

Cocker, Joe, *With a Little Help from my Friends*, Regal Zonophone, 1969.

Deep Purple, *Made in Japan*, Purple, 1972.

Elton John, *Greatest Hits*, DJM, 1974 (compilation).

Holly, Buddy, *20 Golden Greats*, MCA, 1978 (compilation).

Rolling Stones, The, *Story of the Stones*, K-Tel, 1982 (compilation).

Small Faces, The, *Ogden's Nut Gone Flake*, Immediate, 1968.

Small Faces, The, *The Small Faces Collection*, Castle, 1986 (compilation).

Various, *Sgt. Pepper Knew My Father*, NME/Island, 1988.

Index